Bear Bloopers
True Stories

From the Great Smoky Mountains

National Park

By

Carolyn Jourdan

E-book ISBN-13: 978-0-9899304-1-3

Cover Design by Karen Key

Cover photo by Bill Lea http://www.BillLea.com

I am extremely grateful to the following people who generously shared their experiences and allowed this book to come into being:

Rick Varner

Rick Varner has been a Wildlife Biological Technician for 26 years. A former Boy Scout, Backpacker, Mountain Climber, and Marine Corps Infantry Sergeant, he estimates that he's spent a quarter of his life sleeping under canvas, nylon, or the stars. He's hiked over 25,000 miles in the mountains while hunting wild hogs, chasing bears, and building or repairing all the bear-proof food storage cable systems at every campsite and shelter in the Park.

Dwight McCarter

Dwight McCarter served as a Backcountry Ranger in the Great Smoky Mountains National Park for over twenty years and was a lead tracker for the National Park Service. He is the author of several wonderful books about the Smokies, is a force of nature, and a superb speaker. His books are *Lost!*, *Mayday!*, and *Meigs Line*.

Joe Kelly

Joe Kelly is a retired ranger and expert tracker. He teaches a fascinating course on tracking for the Smoky Mountain Field School. He is co-author of the book *Meigs Line* with Dwight McCarter.

George Minnigh

George Minnigh is a retired a Backcountry Ranger who had a 30-year career with the National Park Service. He was the first manager of the entire backcountry in the Great Smoky Mountains National Park where he oversaw 800 miles of trails, 87 backcountry campsites, 15 trail shelters, 70,000-80,000 camper nights per year, and the helicopter rescue of 150 hikers stranded in the backcountry during the blizzard of 1993.

Tom Harrington

Tom Harrington has been a Park volunteer since 2000. A tireless hiker and nature photographer, Tom has hiked every trail on the Tennessee side of the Park. He presents programs about the natural and cultural history of Cades Cove at the Primitive Baptist Church on the Cades Cove Loop Road and at the Cades Cove amphitheater. He also speaks about the Park's wilderness and wildflowers and gives guided tours.

Bill Lea

Bill Lea has been photographing in the Smokies since 1975. More than 7,000 of his photos have been published by Audubon Calendars, BBC Wildlife, Defenders of Wildlife, numerous Great Smoky Mountains Association publications, National Geographic books, Nature Conservancy, National Wildlife, and many others. For the last twenty years Bill has specialized in photographing and documenting bear behavior. He has authored three books including *Cades Cove - Window to a Secret World, Great Smoky Mountains Wildlife Portfolio,* and *The Everglades - Where Wonders Only Whisper*. Bill also leads photographic workshops across the country. For more information please visit www.BillLea.com

Jack Burgin

Jack Burgin is an attorney with Kramer Rayson in Knoxville, TN. Mr. Burgin graduated with honors from The University of Tennessee College of Law in 1989. He is a Past President of Appalachian Bear Rescue and currently serves on its Board of Directors as General Counsel.
www.AppalachianBearRescue.org

Liz Domingue

Liz Domingue has over 25 years of experience as a naturalist, educator, wildlife biologist, photographer, and writer. She received her M.S. in Wildlife Ecology and Conservation Biology from the University of Florida and her B.S. in Wildlife Biology from Cornell University. She is trained in CPR and is certified by The National Registry as a Wilderness First Responder. She designs and leads customized trips, naturalist rambles, and education programs, and delights in meeting people from all walks of life. www.JustGetOutdoors.com

Mark A. Dunaway

Mark A. Dunaway is an Assistant Professor of Biology who specializes in avian communication and nature recordings. He recently published *Soothing Sounds of the Smokies*, provided the recordings for *Bird Songs of the Smokies,* and is currently involved in other publication projects. He is dedicated to educating adults and children about the natural world through speaking engagements and his educational website:
www.TheBiologyZone.com

Marci Dunaway

Marci Dunaway is a Clinical Psychologist and naturalist who, when not practicing psychology, enjoys wildlife and nature photography. She also assists with the development of educational programs and material for wildlife and nature projects.

Kelli Green, Westy Fletcher, John Broome, Carl Gheesling, Joan Nance, and Sharon Ryan

The above-mentioned folks are present or former employees of the Great Smoky Mountains Association. www.SmokiesInformation.org

A handful of the stories in this book are presented anonymously because the people involved didn't want their identities revealed.

***

In this book Smoky Mountain dialect is rendered as it sounds. Appalachian speech is poetic and musical. It's sung as much as spoken, so a significant portion of the meaning is conveyed in the cadences and tones.

Dialect is used in conversation by people of all levels of education and intelligence, so no apostrophes will highlight dropped g's or word variants, as if they are errors. For the same reason, the local grammar is retained.

This was done to enable the reader to experience Smoky Mountain life and language intimately, as an insider would.

Table of Contents

Prologue

This is a collection of hilarious, heartbreaking, and terrifying stories of human encounters with wild black bears in the Great Smoky Mountains National Park.

The stories are wide-ranging in tone and content because they were told to me by people with differing levels of experience handling large wild animals—rangers, scientists, wildlife photographers, wilderness guides, tourists, and others.

These vignettes span a period of more than forty years and half a million acres of forested mountain wilderness. Most of these stories represent the *wrong* thing to do when meeting one of the world famous icons of the Smokies.

Don't try any of this at home (or in the Park).

The New Guy

TO GIVE YOU a sense of the extraordinary personalities of two of the people who contributed stories to this book, Dwight McCarter and Joe Kelly, here's Joe's description of his first encounter with Dwight.

Both of these men had distinguished careers as rangers and trackers for the National Park Service.

Joe Kelly

"When I went to meet Dwight McCarter for the first time, I went to the ranger's kiosk where he was working, but nobody was there, so I waited.

"After awhile I started wandering around and eventually came across a guy laying in the grass on his stomach. He had his ear to the ground, like he was listening to something.

"I stood there watching him for a few moments, then noticed a Stetson ranger hat on the ground nearby. I realized this might be the fellow I was looking for.

"I didn't want to seem ignorant or make any noise, so I laid down and put my ear to the ground, too. After a few minutes of silence, I admitted, 'I can't hear a thing.'

"'I know,' said the ranger. 'It's been like that *all day*!'

"Both of us burst out laughing and then the fellow introduced himself. It was Dwight."

This Restroom Ain't Big Enough for the Both of Us

Dwight McCarter

"I GOT CALLED to go to the parking lot at Elkmont Campground. Somebody needed to deal with a female bear that was in a bad mood. It was close to mating season when even the gentlest bears can get ornery.

"The bear had just ripped the trunk off a Karmann Ghia. She ate the seat and then tore up the inside of the car looking for food.

"At the same time the bear was chewing on anything that had a food smell on it, a couple of maintenance men were cleaning the nearby public restrooms. They finished with the men's room and started moving their equipment around to the women's side.

"First they moved a sign that said *Closed for Cleaning*. They propped it between the doorknob and doorjamb to hold the restroom door ajar. Then they went back to get the rest of their supplies.

"Just as they were returning to the women's side with the last of their gear, they saw a lady walk over from the campground, take the sign down, go inside, then turn around and put the sign back they way they'd had it.

"The workmen stood off to the side, politely waiting for the woman to leave before they resumed their cleaning.

"But before the lady came out, the female bear who'd finished wreaking havoc on the Karmann Ghia came around the corner. As she passed the open door of the restroom, she smelled some food odors coming from the nearly full trashcan inside.

"She decided to investigate further.

"When the bear stuck her snout through the partially open door to get a better whiff of the trashcan, she jostled the sign and knocked it loose.

"It fell and hit her in the head and startled her. She leaped out of the way but, because of the direction she'd been facing, she ended up inside the restroom.

"And because she'd knocked the sign down, the spring-loaded door closed behind her, shutting the creature inside the bathroom, together with the lady.

"The maintenance men immediately got on the radio and called me, saying, 'Dwight … Dwight … There's a lady in the bathroom … and there's a *bear* in there *with* her. Somebody needs to get over here *right now* and save that lady … and the bear!'

"I ran over from my kiosk and stood outside the restroom for a few seconds, listening to see if I could tell what was going on inside, but I couldn't hear anything.

"It was so quiet I could hear a faucet dripping, but that was all.

"I asked the maintenance men, 'Are you sure there's a bear in there?'

"'Yes!' they said.

"'Are you sure there's a woman in there?'

"'Yes!'

"I didn't want to make the situation worse by barging into the restroom and upsetting the bear even more, so I walked around to the side of the building where there was an air vent and bent over and spoke through it in a loud whisper.

"I said, 'Ma'am?'

"There was no answer.

"So I said a little louder, 'Ma'am?'

"The lady must've realized I was trying to talk to her, because an annoyed and suspicious woman's voice said, '*Yes*?'

"'Ma'am, I don't want to alarm you,' I said, 'but I believe there's a bear in the restroom with you.'

"'A *what*?' the voice said.

"'A *bear*.'

"'No there certainly is not!' the woman snapped. She was obviously irritated at what she thought was a prank.

"'Well, Ma'am,' I said, 'I'm a Park ranger, and I'm pretty sure there *is* a bear in there with you. I need you to help me out. Okay? Why don't you look under the partition and let me know what you see.'

"I waited while I hoped the woman was doing what I'd asked her to.

"Then I heard her scream. Apparently she'd just discovered the bear.

"I readied my gun and raced back around the building to the door on the women's side. But before I could get in, the door burst open and a woman holding her pants about three-fourths of the way up her thighs raced out, screaming like a banshee, nearly knocking me down.

"She refused to stop even when I called out to her and she kept running until she disappeared into the woods.

"The maintenance crew came over and stood there with me, staring at the closed door, contemplating the situation.

"A wild bear is attracted to the smell of lollipops and milkshakes and the other sorts of food scraps that are in trashcans, but it will normally be afraid of humans. This bear's unexpected encounter with the sign, the door, and the hysterical woman was bound to have frightened it.

"The bear's instinct, just like the woman's, would be to run away into the woods as fast as possible. And, in fact, the bear was trying to do just that, but a bear can't turn a doorknob. She was trapped inside a concrete block building on the wrong side of a door that would have to be pulled open from the bear's side.

"The maintenance men and I listened to the bear clawing up the interior of the restroom, trying to find a way out. The racket got louder as the bear got more frantic.

"Something had to be done.

"I grabbed a mop in one hand and held my gun in the other, and hopped up on the two-foot retaining wall beside the door. I told the maintenance guys to turn the doorknob. I told them if they'd get the door unlatched, I'd take care of the rest and get the bear out of there somehow.

"My plan was to give the guys time to back up, then shove the door open with the mop handle, and stand back, and hope the bear would come out on her own. I failed to tell the men they should run for their lives immediately after turning the knob.

"The *instant* they turned the doorknob, the bear pried the door open the rest of the way and came roaring out. The maintenance men bolted toward the woods with the bear right behind them. I don't think the bear was chasing them as much as they all just happened to be running in the same direction.

"The inside of the restroom was a wreck. The trapped bear had destroyed nearly everything but the concrete walls.

"Eventually the woman and the maintenance men came back out of the woods. But the bear was never seen again.

"The Park Service held a safety meeting after the incident. There was a pretty hot debate about who was at fault for all the damage to the restroom. The maintenance crew and I tried to blame it on each other. Nobody blamed the woman or the bear."

**

Tourist: "Where do we sign up to ride those horses?"

Ranger: "Those aren't horses, they're elk."

Tourist: "Where do we sign up to ride those elk?"

Bear Hug

Joe Kelly

"I WAS THE RANGER on duty, driving a Park Service pickup truck on patrol through a popular picnic area one afternoon when I came across something that was so unbelievable, at first I couldn't understand what I was seeing.

"It looked like a woman was slow dancing with a bear.

"A full-grown black bear was standing up on its hind legs and had one paw on each of the woman's shoulders.

"I thought I was gonna lose my mind—and she was gonna lose her life.

"When I got closer, I realized the woman was feeding the bear vanilla wafers by holding them between her teeth. The bear was leaning forward, putting his snout point blank into the woman's face, and taking the cookies from her mouth with his.

"He stood there, embracing her, while he chewed the cookies. He had her literally in a *bear hug*.

"The woman was happily repeating the procedure with one cookie after another while her family photographed her and a large crowd looked on.

"Everybody was having a good time, except for me. All I could do was pray.

"I said, *Oh Lord, please don't let that woman run out of vanilla wafers!*

"As carefully as I could I eased my vehicle up closer to where the woman was standing.

"When the bear saw my green truck, he flinched. Obviously this wasn't his first encounter with a ranger. The bear knew there

8

was someone inside the truck who'd seen him doing something he wasn't supposed to be doing.

"Some of the tamer bears knew not only how to recognize a Park Service vehicle, but also a ranger uniform, or even *particular rangers*!

"The bear shoved himself back away from the lady, accidentally knocking her down. Then he ran off into the woods.

"Thank heavens it's rare for our black bears to hurt anyone. The most common injury tourists get from a bear encounter in the Smokies is what they do to themselves and each other while running away. People get hurt in their panicked stampede to escape: twisting ankles, slamming into trees, tearing through briars, and running into each other.

"These situations can seem sorta comical, but it can all go terribly wrong in an instant. Some people don't understand that these animals are *wild*. Others don't understand what *wild* means."

Anybody In the Area?

RICK VARNER is the stuff of legend for his heroic, hands-on interventions with wild animals. Several of his escapades are chronicled in Kim DeLozier's *Bear in the Back Seat* series. Rick is a former Marine and it shows.

He's risked his life more than once to save tourists and other rangers from tough situations. But at least once, he accidentally caused a bear blooper.

Rick Varner

"My first year working in the Park I caught a great big bear in a hog trap right next to the Appalachian Trail.

"Then the next day I caught him again.

"In fact, I caught the same bear, in the same trap, for six days in a row.

"This bear was an unusually large and strong animal, and he could've torn his way out of the trap if he'd wanted to, but every day he waited peacefully for me to come by and open the door to let him out.

"He wasn't aggressive. He just loved the corn we used as bait to lure wild hogs into the trap.

"Whenever I got there and opened the door for him, he'd just walk out real calmly and head off into the woods. And if I didn't arrive at exactly the same time as the day before, he'd look at me like *it's about time you got here.*

"After the sixth day in a row, I realized there was no point in using that particular trap anymore, so I gave up and stopped baiting it.

"For some reason, that particular bear wasn't at all traumatized by getting caught in the trap. I guess the way he saw it, once he got locked inside, he could enjoy a leisurely meal without worrying about any other animals bothering him or trying to take the food away from him.

"When you're about to release a bear from a trap that's built like these traps were, the first thing you did was put a rock on top of the little opening that's made in the top of the trap. It's an escape hatch for small animals that get caught in the trap by mistake, but the hole is big enough for a bear to reach through and scratch you, so you need to block it.

"After I covered the escape hatch with a rock, I'd jump up on top of the trap and open the door from above. I never had a bear turn back and try to come after me when I opened the door because they're always so glad to get out, they take off for the woods immediately.

Or almost always. You can never take anything for granted when dealing with wild animals.

"A couple of months later, I found a different hog trap with a different bear sitting inside it eating the corn bait. I opened the door as usual, but this bear totally ignored me.

"He wasn't through eating.

"I wanted the critter to get out of the trap, so I got a stick and started beating on the metal door, screaming as loud as I could. Well, that scared the bear and he bolted out of the cage.

"He ran downhill about fifty yards until he reached the Appalachian Trail, then he turned and took off down the path.

"Bears are like people in that they prefer to do things the easy way. Why go crashing through the woods, and having to sidehill on a steep mountainside when there's a relatively flat trail nearby?

"The fleeing bear charged down the Appalachian Trail and a few seconds later I heard screaming.

"The Appalachian Trail is not very wide. The bear stayed on it and ran right through the middle of a group of six girls who were hiking.

"No one was hurt. The bear totally ignored the girls, but he'd brushed against a couple of them to pass them on the narrow trail.

"Getting jostled by a large, stampeding wild bear made quite an impression on the girls. And me.

"Ever since that happened, before I release a bear, I always call out, *Anybody in the area?*"

***

Tourist: "How high do you have to get before the deer turn into elk?"

Ranger: "High on what?"

Tourist: "I mean elevation."

Ranger: "What?"

Tourist: "At what elevation will a deer become an elk?"

R & R

Anonymous

"ONE FALL during the peak of the change of leaf color in the Smokies, I was stressed out and needed a break so I rented a chalet on a high ridge on the edge of the Park.

"I went there by myself to rest, relax, and enjoy nature for a few days before all the hustle and bustle of the holidays got going. I made a special point of reserving a cabin with a hot tub that had a fabulous view.

"When I got there, I unpacked as quickly as I could. I was really looking forward to getting into that hot tub for a long soak and enjoy the sunset over the mountains. I changed and grabbed a towel, and headed for the tub.

"As soon as I went out onto the deck I immediately sensed something wasn't right. I did a double take on the hot tub and was shocked to see that someone was already in it!

"Then I looked more carefully and saw it wasn't some*one*, but some*thing*. An adult black bear was sitting in the hot tub, obviously enjoying itself.

"I dropped my towel and screamed and ran back inside the house.

"Apparently I scared the bear, because it jumped out of the hot tub and took off. I was totally freaked out, but decided I shouldn't let the bear ruin my holiday. The mountains were the bear's home anyway, not mine.

"So I went back outside, made sure the bear was gone, and intended to get into the hot tub. That's when I noticed the surface of the water was covered with a thick layer of black hair. The water was filthy and looked more like a witch's caldron than a spa.

"This was a *very* unwelcome discovery. It was all I could do not to cry. I kept telling myself to think positive. I scooped *many* handfuls of hair out of the tub, tossed out a few leaves and twigs, then gave the rim a good scrubbing.

"By the time I finished, it was almost full dark. The water still didn't look clean though, so I couldn't bring myself to get in. And I knew it would take a long time to empty and clean and refill the tub.

"I was so tired at this point, I decided to tackle all that tomorrow. I went back inside and sat at the kitchen table in the dark, staring out at the last traces of the sunset.

"A few minutes later I saw a large black shape making its way slowly toward the chalet from the woods. The looming shadow came to the edge of the porch, paused, then crept up to the hot tub, climbed over the edge, and settled in.

"It was the bear again.

"I watched the animal's obvious pleasure at sitting in the warm tub after a hard day in the woods. I tried to imagine how exhausted the creature must be from scouring the forest all day, trying to find enough acorns to stay alive during its long winter nap.

"I'd come to the mountains to see nature and here it was. So, I decided to let the critter stay. I went to bed and left the bear to enjoy the hot tub in peace."

How Far Can a Ranger Fly?

Rick Varner

"BEFORE WE HAD transfer cages made especially for bears, we used to transport them inside wild hog traps that had been slightly modified.

"Jerry-rigged hog traps aren't really suitable because they're made out of chain link fencing. A bear cage needs to have a smooth, slick floor, so we can slide a big, heavy bear into it and lay the animal out safely for travel.

"A cage with a wire bottom creates problems for positioning bears because they're sedated when we're moving them. It's a real chore to get a heavy bear into a position so we're sure they can breathe well while they're unconscious.

"One time we were moving a 300-pound male bear. He was immobilized with drugs and as we wrestled him into the hog trap, his claws kept snagging against the wire bottom of the cage, so he lay there crumpled up in an awkward position.

"I needed to get inside the cage and maneuver the bear so he'd be able to breathe freely. The cage was in the back of a pickup truck and the only opening was on the top, and was on hinges.

"I had a young fellow from the Student Conservation Association helping me. I asked him to hold the lid of the cage open when I climbed inside to stretch the bear out.

"I was tugging on the heavy critter, dragging 300 pounds of floppy dead weight along on the chain link, when suddenly the bear raised his head.

"Uh oh. That wasn't good.

"That was *really* not good.

"The bear was waking up, even though I desperately needed him to stay asleep at least while I was in the cage with him!

"I got worried that the kid who was supposed to be holding the cage door open for me, might panic and drop the lid and lock me inside with the bear.

"Either way, I needed to do something fast.

"At the same moment I realized I needed get out of the cage, the bear snapped his teeth *right in my face*, nearly point blank! So I did the only thing I could.

"I put all the leg strength I had into making a flat-footed leap outta there. I dived straight over the top of the bear toward the gap of the partially-open cage door.

"Thank goodness the intern didn't flinch much. He held the top open wide enough for me to get through.

"As I went soaring through the air, I looked down to see what the bear was doing. I can still see the whole sequence of events in my mind—it was like watching a slow motion movie.

"I went flying out of the cage like Superman, and as I did, the bear swiveled his head swiveled around, following me. He snapped his big jaws over and over, trying to bite me, but each time he snapped, his teeth were chomping down on the place where I'd been just a second before.

"He was snapping about an inch behind where I actually was. If he hadn't been a little groggy, he would've *eaten me up*!

"I went sailing out of the cage, which was good, but then I kept going, and that turned out to be not as good. I cleared the cage, and then the tailgate of the pickup, and kept right on hurtling through the air.

"Once I was airborne with that much momentum, there was nothing I could do but ride it out. There was nothing for me to grab, so my acrobatics ended with a high-speed face-plant onto the asphalt parking lot.

"Lemme tell ya, hitting the asphalt face-first, *hurt*. But not nearly as much as that bear's teeth would've!

"So, if anybody ever wonders how far a ranger can fly, the answer is *as far as they need to!*"

I Need to Get My BEARings

Dwight McCarter

"AS PART OF HIS course work, a graduate student at the University of Tennessee was sent out into the backcountry to locate and assess the condition of a particular bear that was hibernating in the Smokies.

"The bear was wearing a radio collar that broadcasted on a distinctive frequency. That way the signal could be identified as belonging to a specific bear and the bear could be found.

"The student drove to the Park and hiked into the backcountry toward where the bear's territory was historically known to be. When he thought he might be getting close, he turned on the special tracking device that monitored the bear collars and tuned it to the frequency of the bear he was looking for.

"He instantly got a very strong signal. That was a big relief because it meant he was already close to the bear he was looking for.

"The young man walked around, trying to spot a den, but he couldn't find it. The radio signal continued to indicate he was very close, but couldn't see a den anywhere.

"It was maddening. He thrashed around in the woods for hours, getting more and more frustrated, going round and round in circles, but couldn't locate the bear.

"Finally he gave up, exhausted, and returned to the university. He contacted his professor and told him what had happened.

"The professor asked the student to take a look in his backpack. He'd been carrying an extra collar in case he needed to change out the one on the bear he was studying. The teacher asked the student to see if the backup collar was switched *on*.

"It was.

"The student checked the central logbook and confirmed that the spare collar he'd been carrying broadcasted on a frequency close to that of the collar he'd been trying to locate.

"So, he'd spent the better part of a long hard day tracking his own backpack through the wilderness. And he'd never found it."

***

Tourist: "How old do deer have to be before they turn into elk?"

Surprise!

Rick Varner

"THE MOST SCARED I've ever been of a bear happened when I wasn't even sure it *was* a bear.

"I was walking the Appalachian Trail at night hunting pigs when I got a strange feeling and something made me stop. I didn't know what it was that made me hold still, but I got the idea that I should.

"It was pitch black. I stood there, listening really hard. I could hear something that sounded like heavy breathing.

"I listened some more and then I heard scraping noises coming from about six feet away. I couldn't see anything so I reached for the light on my shotgun and started backing up.

"I heard a snort, then something let out a big breath, blowing and huffing, and clicked its teeth. Then I heard a really hard slap against some wood about three or four feet away.

"Whatever it was, it was getting closer. Then something hit the trail right at my feet. That was *really* scary.

"I was dancing around in the dark, trying to get my light turned on. It was a twelve-volt tractor headlight powered by a fifteen-pound battery I was carrying in my backpack.

"A power cord ran from the backpack to the light and the rig was awkward to operate. When I finally got the on, I saw a 300-pound bear standing right next to me, reared up on his hind legs, and a dead tree limb was at my feet.

"The noises were being caused by the bear. He was trying to warn me that he was there. He'd slapped the trunk of a tree real hard to let me know, and his slap made a dead limb fall out of the tree.

"I'd almost bolted and run away in the dark, without even knowing what was going on. Too much was happening at once, it was impossible to sort it all out when I couldn't see anything.

"I'm glad I stopped when I first got the feeling I should hold still. I was lucky. I wouldn't have wanted to accidentally run into a bear in a situation like that."

Stark Terror at the Mailbox

Kelli Green

WHEN I WAS hired by the Great Smoky Mountains Association, I had no idea how easy it was to encounter a bear in the Park. Everyone in and around Park Headquarters had at least one scary bear story from their own personal experience.

At first the tales of man versus bear were dramatic and thrilling, but over time then they started to genuinely scare me and I tried to avoid hearing any more of them.

The sheer number of bear stories gradually had the effect of causing me to write myself a mental note that said: *Do not go into the woods.*

Kelli Green, of the GSMA Human Resources and Accounting departments, had a particularly memorable encounter.

"I was nine months pregnant," she said, "and waddled outside to get the mail.

"I pulled an armload of letters and packages out of the box and got a glimpse of something big and black out of the corner of my eye. It was a bear standing at the base of a tree about ten feet away.

"It scared me to death. My brain was screaming, *Run!! Run!!!*

"But I knew from being told so many times, *The one thing you must never do is run!!*

"So I stood there, paralyzed.

"I was so pregnant and so loaded down with mail, I wasn't sure I could outrun the bear even for the few yards it would take to get to the front door.

"I didn't dare move and I didn't dare look directly at the bear, for fear of accidentally challenging it and making it charge. I stood there for so long I started getting tired and sorta dizzy.

"I waited and waited for the bear to leave, but it wouldn't! Finally, one of the teaching rangers came around the corner of the building and said, 'Hey Kelli, how's it goin?'

"I started to warn him about the bear, but before I could say anything, he walked right up to it and grabbed hold of it! And picked it up!

"I was totally in shock. It's a wonder I didn't go into labor right then."

Wow, I thought as I listened to Kelli's story, I knew the rangers were much braver than me, but this was *really* impressive. How heroic that a young ranger would risk his own life to save a pregnant woman. I wanted to swoon in awe of his courage.

Then Kelli said, "I turned toward the ranger and that's when I really saw the bear for the first time. It was a life-size black plastic bear that they use for outdoor demonstrations in front of large groups. He'd left it propped against the tree while he went inside to get something from his office.

"I'd been given the scare of my life by a *plastic* bear!"

Whew. At first I was relieved, then amused, and then sorta irritated to realize the bear was fake. So the ranger hadn't been brave or sacrificing himself, had he? He hadn't been killed, or mauled, or even scared. In fact, it was his fault the whole thing had happened in the first place. You'd think a ranger would have more sense than to leave a fake bear standing around in the woods where it could scare people.

For reasons I can't explain, even though this bear story didn't involve a real attack and didn't even involve a real bear, I made another mental note. This one said: *Stay away from the mailbox.*

***

Tourist: "Where's this park everybody keeps talkin' about? We've been drivin' and drivin' and can't find it.

Ranger: "You're in it right now."

Tourist: "Where?"

The Right to BEAR Arms, or Arm Bears

Rick Varner

"ONE YEAR bad weather caused a terrible mast failure in the Park. *Mast* is the word for the natural foods produced in a forest for the wild animals to eat. *Soft mast* is the fruits and berries that ripen in the earlier part of the year and *hard mast* is the acorns and nuts that come later.

"The oak trees produced very few acorns. When this happens, it's really tough on the bears who're trying hard during the last couple of months in the fall to get enough calories to survive during hibernation.

"That year a lot of starving bears left the Park looking for food. It was a disaster. *Two hundred* bears got hit on the roads outside the Park.

"This resulted in a lot of orphaned cubs. And because of the awful food conditions, these orphans were very under-weight. They weighed around twelve pounds in October, which is what they should've weighed in March or May.

"I was furloughed from being a ranger that fall and winter because the Park Service ran out of money. Tennessee Wildlife Resources Agency offered me a job helping out with the orphan cubs.

"Right after I started my new job, someone called to report a cub that had been up in a tree for four days, starving. The mother was obviously dead. So, I went to a wildlife biologist and asked what I should do with the critter.

"I was pretty upset. This was before Appalachian Bear Rescue was created.

"I didn't want all these orphaned cubs to be euthanized, so I decided to try and care for as many of them as I could over the winter.

"I started collecting cubs. I decided to keep only female cubs because I figured that would be the best way to help the bear population survive. In all, I had eight of them.

"I wanted to raise them to be able to survive in the wild, so they had minimal human contact. I never spoke to them, and I fed them through a special opening where they couldn't see me. The cubs had no idea where their food was coming from.

"I got a bunch of wild hog traps to keep the cubs in and I tried as best I could to feed them natural bear foods. I spent two days raking acorns from private land, tossing them onto a net frame I'd stretched across the bed of my pickup truck to act like a sieve, so the acorns would drop into the bed of the truck while the sticks and leaves would be kept out.

"It was hard work, but I was able to fill an entire pickup bed with good white oak acorns. That's a high quality food for bears.

"Then I bought the highest fat content dog food I could, to supplement the acorns, and I foraged vegetables from dumpsters, back when that was still allowed.

"The cubs got fat. They weren't normal height and weight, though. Instead they were short and round like bowling balls because there was no room for them to exercise where I was keeping them penned. But I succeeded in getting their weight up, giving them a reserve to survive on.

"By January there were several that weighed 60-65 pounds, so they were ready to be taken to their dens.

"I released them to known denning areas. A lot of bear den locations in the Smokies have been mapped because of the University of Tennessee's research work.

"Bears won't normally reuse the same den year after year, so I knew there was a good likelihood that some of the known dens would be vacant.

"My idea was to feed the cubs up to a good weight and then stuff them into an old unoccupied den during a cold night and hope they'd stay put until spring.

"I knew that bears would sometimes move around before they were fully awake, before their brain was functioning well, so I knew I'd need to block the entrance of the den so no light would be visible to the little cubs when they woke up from the tranquilizers, or they might try to climb out. They could fall or get lost and not be able to find their den again. If that happened, they'd die, so I planned to use sticks and leaves to close the entrance.

"When one of the 65-pound cubs was sedated, I filled a burlap sack with its bedding so it would have a familiar smell in its new den. A friend and I carried the cub up a hill, intending to put him in a den inside a hollow log. The log was damp at the opening, but twenty feet down inside it, at the other end of the log, it was snug and dry.

"I didn't want to just roll the sedated cub down into the far end. I wanted to place him in a good position, butt first, and leave him facing the right way to crawl out in the spring. The surface of the inside the log was rough though, so I had to climb inside it with the bear and slide him backwards in little increments down toward the bottom of the hole.

"Just as I got him into a good position deep inside the log, the cub started to moan. That was not an ideal situation. It meant the animal was waking up.

"I immediately tried to back up, but I couldn't. The inside of the log was snagging my clothes on all sides. It was pitch black down in there, too.

"My face was right in the bear's face. The cub was moaning and starting to move—and I was stuck.

"I got out my pocket knife and locked the blade open. I jammed it into the wood and tried to use it as a handhold to shove myself backwards, toward the exit.

"I couldn't see the bear at all, but I could hear him really well. My friend, who was standing at the den's entrance wondering what was going on, was blocking what little light there was.

"I needed to move backwards fifteen to twenty feet pretty fast, but it was tough going. I'd shoved myself a fair distance, when suddenly, and without any warning at all, I went flying backwards out of the hollow log.

"My friend realized I'd been down there long enough for the cub to start waking up and, as soon as he could see enough of my legs to get a good grip on me, he jerked me out by the ankles.

"My exit happened so fast, and forcefully, and unexpectedly, I let go of my knife. I didn't mean to, but I'd left it inside the log.

"In the spring I went back to try to retrieve my knife, but there'd been a huge windstorm in the interim and there were a lot of trees blown down in the area. I couldn't find the log we'd put the cub in."

***

Ever since Rick told me this story I've been worried about a hungry young orphan bear cub being left alone out there in the woods with access to a knife.

Even now as I'm writing this book, I sometimes glance out the window and wonder if somewhere out there wandering around in the Park is a bear that's armed and dangerous.

***

Please Kill the Bear!

Rick Varner

"THE LARGE NUMBER of bears leaving the Park during that terrible winter to look for food was causing a lot of problems and we were often called to go get a bear and move it away from someone's house.

"Whenever I showed up at a house to get a bear, people who saw me, especially kids, would beg me, *Please don't hurt the bear!*

"I had a canned speech I gave to reassure the spectators and explain what I was doing. I gave it about a hundred times a month.

"Only once did something totally different happen. I was called to deal with a problem bear in Townsend. When I arrived, a little girl came running up to me, crying and flailing with her hands. She plowed into me.

"It's okay little girl," I said. "I'm not gonna hurt the bear. I'm gonna take him to a place where it's easier for him to stay out of trouble.

"But instead of being reassured she shocked me by saying, 'I *want* you to hurt the bear. I want you to *kill* that bear!'

"The starving bear had just eaten four of her 4-H rabbits.

"I felt bad for the little girl, but I just relocated the bear. I didn't kill it."

***

Tourist: "What time do they turn off the waterfalls?"

Ranger: "They don't turn em off."

Tourist: "Well when do they turn em on?"

Ranger: "They pretty much stay on."

Tourist: "You leave em on all the time? Day and night?"

Ranger: "Yep."

A Ticklish Situation

Dwight McCarter

"BEARS' NOSES are some of the most sensitive on earth. They can sniff out food across great distances. One of their favorite smells is of frying meat, especially bacon. Bears love bacon grease so much, they'll even go after an empty cast iron skillet if it's been used a lot.

"One summer a family from Indiana was visiting the Park and staying at the Cosby Campground. The mother of the family, Mary, was an excellent cook. She and her husband, George, got along really well and had a habit of tickling each other.

"One morning Mary was up early cooking up a nice big breakfast for her family. She was bent over an outdoor fire, frying bacon.

"A bear smelled the food and waddled up behind her while she worked.

"The bear got so carried away by the smell of the bacon cooking in all that delicious grease, he couldn't help himself—he gave Mary a nudge to move her out of the way. That was his way of asking for the skillet.

"Mary kept her eyes on the sizzling bacon and didn't bother turning around. She said in a playful way, "Oh George, quit that!"

"The bear waited a moment, then gave her another nudge.

"Still not turning around, she said, "George, I *mean* it—*quit* that! I'm trying to cook!"

"The third time the bear nudged her, Mary lost her patience and swatted the air behind her. She didn't hit anything because

35

she wasn't looking where she was slapping. Instead she was turning the bacon it as it browned.

"The bear was even more annoyed than Mary. He slapped back at her. And he had the benefit of being able to see what he was doing, so he made contact, swatting her in the butt.

"This was too much. Mary'd had enough. She spun around to give her husband a piece of her mind, but it was immediately obvious that it wasn't George getting frisky with her—it was a full grown wild black bear.

"She let out a blood-curdling scream, dropped her spatula, and ran off—which was just what the bear had been hoping for. He instantly went for the bacon.

"Mary's scream brought George awake and he scrambled out of their tent to find a bear gobbling up what was supposed to have been the family breakfast.

"Being a good husband, he chased the bear away and saved what remained of the family bacon.

"Then went looking for his wife."

Nodding Off

Anonymous

"MY BROTHER and I were headed to Mt. LeConte and I was hiking faster, so we became separated on the trail. I got pretty far ahead of him.

"Near the top of the mountain, I came to a place with a nice view that seemed like a good place to wait for my brother. I took my gear off and lay down, using my backpack as a pillow.

"I didn't mean to, but I dozed off. I roused when I could hear my brother coming up the trail. I mumbled something to him without opening my eyes, but he didn't answer me.

"Then a minute later I said something else. I was still groggy, but gradually coming more awake. He still didn't respond, but I didn't think anything about it because he's a quiet guy.

"Then, when I could tell he was standing right next to me, I spoke for a third time and then I opened my eyes.

"A momma bear and two cubs were looming over me.

"I was so groggy, I wasn't exactly afraid, but I knew it was a real bad idea to be that close to a wild bear, especially a mother with cubs, so I hopped up and backed away from them.

"Unfortunately, I couldn't go far because I was at the edge of a cliff. That's why there was such a nice view.

"I was sorta trapped there, but figured I better find a way to leave, so I climbed down the cliff about a hundred feet and then traversed sideways until I thought I was out of the bears' way and then climbed back up onto the trail.

"My brother eventually showed up and we went together to retrieve my backpack.

"We found it, but it was shredded into ribbons. The bears had eaten all the food in it, and the pack and all its contents were ripped to pieces, even a metal canteen that had been filled with water.

"It was amazing to see what was left of my gear and understand how strong a bear's teeth and jaws and claws had to be to turn both fabric and metal into spaghetti."

UnBEARable

Anonymous

"ONE OF MY friends is a lady who lives by herself in a cabin near the edge of the Park. She has a big furry black Chow dog that she's just crazy about. The dog's name is *Bear*.

"One evening at dusk, she called the dog to come in, but he didn't come when she called him. When it got full dark, she called again, but the dog still wouldn't come in.

"This was very unusual, so she went outside in her nightgown and walked around the edge of the yard, calling for her dog in the dark. At the far edge of her lawn, next to the woods, she finally spotted him sniffing at something.

"She said, 'Bear, come here!' But he didn't mind her. This made her mad.

"She stomped over to the dog and gave him a good scolding. Then she grabbed for his collar, intending to drag him inside, but she couldn't feel it.

"This mad her even madder because she thought he'd lost the collar, and it was an expensive leather one, custom made with his name engraved on a brass label.

"She grabbed a handful of hair and pulled at the scruff of his neck a few times, trying to force the dog toward the house with no success. Then she realized his fur felt sorta different. It felt stiffer than usual.

"Then she looked at the creature more carefully and realized the animal she was trying to drag into the house wasn't *Bear* the dog, but was an actual bear—a wild black bear.

"She let go of the bear and ran back into her house. Fortunately the bear was a good sport. It didn't bother to chase her, but simply continued to graze on the white oak acorns at the edge of the yard.

"When the bear finished foraging, it wandered away. Soon after that, *Bear* the dog came to the door and wanted in.

"Wiser than his master, the dog had stayed out of sight until the bear left."

The Bucket of Chicken

Dwight McCarter

"BEARS HAVE A WINDOW of six to eight months a year to consume all the calories they're gonna need to survive for the whole winter. How much time they have depends on how early foodstuffs emerge in the spring and how soon the cold weather arrives in the winter.

"The early months in the spring are always a tough time for hungry bears that have emerged from their dens, because it takes a while before the best edible plants, like berries, are available. And then, to make matters worse, in some years the fall acorn crop is poor, so the last few months that are so crucial for fattening up are lean, as well.

"This is why it's important for a bear to eat as much as it can, whenever it can. It never knows what the future will offer in terms of food.

"In addition to being highly motivated to locate anything edible, bears are said to be even smarter than dogs. And they have excellent memories. They learn quickly how to home in on calories.

"This ability to find food was vividly demonstrated to a family who bought a bucket of chicken and sides of baked beans and potato salad at a drive-thru on their way into the Park. They planned to have it for lunch, but before starting their picnic they pulled off at a parking lot and locked their Volkswagen Beetle while they took a short hike to work up an appetite.

"Unbeknownst to them, a hungry bear was foraging nearby. He smelled the chicken and used his great strength to tear into the VW and eat everything. Then wandered off into the woods.

"That bucket of chicken was so delicious it made a very strong impression on the bear. So, the next time he saw a VW Beetle in the same parking lot, he broke into it, and tore it apart looking for the chicken. Unfortunately there wasn't any.

"They hadn't done it on purpose, but the previous family had trained that bear to think of a VW Beetle as nothing more than a large bucket of fried chicken.

"After this second incident, the rangers decided to capture and relocate the bear to a remote area of the Park, far away from temptation, so he'd be able to live a normal life in the wild and not present any further danger to people or cars. This strategy worked well and the bear didn't cause any more trouble.

"Please remember when you're visiting the Park: don't do anything that will cause a bear to see your car (or anyone else's) as an extra-large cooler or an easy-to-open dumpster."

Crackers

George Minnigh

"WE TELL PEOPLE in as many ways as possible—in person, with signs, with leaflets. It's even printed on the maps:

Warning, do not cook or eat in the shelter.

Food odors attract bears.

or

Warning, do not cook or eat in the sleeping area.

Food odors attract bears.

"But some people just don't get it and they cause a lot of problems.

"I'll see people camping in the shelters along the Appalachian Trail and warn them in person and they'll act like they understand, but if I come back ten minutes later I'll find them laying on the bunks inside the shelter eating crackers.

"I was up there in the first place because we'd gotten reports that a bear was causing trouble. This sort of behavior was the reason. It's frustrating to try to deal with. Misbehaving people lead to misbehaving bears."

You Fellas Need a Ride?

Dwight McCarter

"HEADQUARTERS got a call in the middle of the night saying gunshots had been heard in an area of the Park near where I live, so Dispatch called me at home and asked me to go check it out. The place I was sent to was between my house and the office, so I drove my own vehicle—a beat up old pickup truck.

"I drove slow along the section of road where the shots had been heard, looking for any signs of activity. I came to a long curve and slowed down even more. Then, at the tightest part of the curve, I was nearly stopped while I scanned the edges of the woods on both sides for any movement.

"To my surprise, two men dressed in dark clothes slid down a steep embankment on the other side of the road, loped over toward me, and hopped into the back of my truck!

"I looked through the back window at the two men, and they looked at me, and we both realized at the same time that they'd made a mistake!

"Apparently they'd been laying up on that bank watching the road, and when I came along moving so slow, they'd mistakenly thought I was the getaway driver who'd been sent to fetch them.

"I stopped my truck and the men made a move to jump out.

"I lifted the rifle I had on the seat beside me and said, 'Fellows, I'm a ranger and I've got a rifle. Don't make me use it.'

"They sat back down.

"I drove them to a law enforcement ranger station where they were arrested on suspicion of poaching. Once they'd been taken into custody, we went back to the area where I'd first seen them, this time in an official Park Service vehicle.

"We found their guns and the body of the bear they'd shot hidden in a culvert near the place where they'd jumped into the back of my truck.

"None of the decisions those fellows made was wise, except to behave while I took them to jail."

How EmBEARrassing

Dwight McCarter

"I WAS HELPING some scientists who were examining a sedated bear.

"They were speaking softly and moving carefully as they performed their procedures, to keep from stimulating the bear, so it would stay asleep.

"But despite their precautions, during the weighing process, the scale got jostled and it made a sharp metal-on-metal clanging noise.

"The racket was loud enough and startling enough to rouse the bear instantly. The animal turned his head and clamped his jaws down on the nearest target—the knee of the closest biologist.

"The good news was that the burst of adrenaline lasted only a second and the drugs took hold again, paralyzing the bear and sending him back to sleep.

"The bad news was that the bear was unconscious in a new position, with his jaws still firmly clamped onto the scientist's knee. If you've ever gotten a good look at a bear's jaws and teeth, you know how delicate this situation was.

"It took two men to pry the critter's mouth loose.

"Luckily, the bear hadn't been able to finish the bite he'd started, so the scientist didn't suffer any serious injuries.

"But it was an extremely scary looking situation for a few minutes."

Lord, Please Don't Let Me Die *This* Way!

Bill Lea

WILDLIFE PHOTOGRAPHERS see many unexpected things. Some of it's interesting, some of it's funny, and some of it's charming enough to make a nice photograph.

But a small percentage of it's ... well ... let's just say they're lucky to live through some of it.

Bill Lea, a famous wildlife photographer who loves to take pictures of bears and the Smokies, says the closest call he ever had in the lower 48 states was in Cades Cove.

"One September," he said, "I was watching a black bear that had climbed up into a white oak tree.

"It was during a time when the Park Service kept cattle in the cove. The bear was up in a tree that still had its leaves, so there was no opportunity to get a usable photo.

"But I really like bears, so I was standing there watching him, just enjoying the scene, not even standing particularly close to the tree, when suddenly the bear flew down the tree, hit the ground, and ran off into the woods.

"I wondered, *what in the world made the bear do that*?

"I glanced around and didn't see anything. Then I thought maybe I heard something and I turned to look directly behind me.

"*Uh oh* ... now I understood why the bear had scampered off.

"A herd of cows was behind me. And they were stampeding toward the bear. Unfortunately, I was standing by myself in the middle of the open field between the bear and the cows.

"I realized the cows were charging the bear to chase him away from where they were grazing. A single cow can't run a bear off, but a whole herd can. These cows had figured out how to work as a group to protect their calves. They'd learned to stampede together to chase bears out of the area.

"I'm ashamed to admit it, but during what could've been my last moments on earth, the only thought that went through my mind was, *This is going to look really pathetic. The headline in the newspapers will read:* Wildlife Photographer Killed by *Cows*!

"That was *not* the way I wanted to go out, or to be remembered, but there wasn't much I could do. So, I wrapped myself around my tripod, hugged my camera equipment, closed my eyes, and tried to stand still.

"It was terrifying. The herd went thundering by, all around me. The ground was shaking with all of them running and I could barely breathe for all the dust they were churning up.

"At some point I realized the cows were going by me on both sides really, really close, but they weren't trampling me.

"When it seemed like maybe they'd all gone past me, I opened my eyes. But there was so much dust in the air I couldn't see *anything*. All I could do was wait, clutching my cameras.

"When the dust finally settled, I was amazed to discover that I was still alive.

"I guess the moral of that story is that the most serious dangers can sometimes come from unexpected critters!"

Here She Comes!

Rick Varner

"WE GOT A REPORT late in the evening saying a cub was caught in a hog trap between Gatlinburg and Twin Creeks. The momma bear was there with the cub, but she was on the outside of the trap.

"Jim Cahill, a law enforcement ranger was the first to arrive at the scene. He saw the momma bear standing on top of the trap, protecting her cub.

"Kim DeLozier and I got there next. We approached the cage and the momma bluff charged us—pretended to attack us to try to scare us away. We threw sticks at her and she ran up a nearby tree and was clinging there, about six feet off the ground, watching us.

"I asked Kim to hold her there up in that tree while I let the cub out. I went to the trap and opened the door wide, but the cub didn't come out. He was at the back of the cage, turned the wrong way, facing his momma.

"I propped the door open and used a stick to try to get the cub to come out, but he wouldn't. Instead he was fighting with the stick. He was just a little fifteen-to-twenty pounder, so I crawled into the trap and pulled him out by scruff and tossed him toward his momma.

"The cub didn't run toward his mother, but instead ran off at an angle. We knew his momma would find him though, so we were done.

"We headed back to our vehicle and when we got near a steep bank, Cahill suddenly screamed, 'Oh my God! Here she comes!' Then he ran away.

"Kim and I both took off in a panic. We tore the bank apart scrambling up it, trying to get away from that momma bear.

"We didn't know it, but the bear was actually still up in a tree. Cahill was just pulling a prank on us. He hadn't really run away either, he'd just ducked out of sight behind his cruiser, screamed out his fake warning, and watched us make fools of ourselves."

One Giant Leap

Mark Dunaway

MARK DUNAWAY is a bird biologist. He spends a lot of time in the Park recording natural bird sounds in the wild. This is not an easy job.

To get good recordings, he's had to develop the ability to sit quietly, without moving, for long periods of time. He's also had to learn how to make himself invisible to animals. Over the years, he's gotten pretty good at it.

When he works he wears a very elaborate 3-D camouflage outfit called a ghillie suit. It has floppy leaves sewn onto it, like the camo worn by military snipers. Mark's wife, Marci, completed his look by sewing cloth leaves all over his headphones.

Mark's work is done mostly at dawn and at dusk, since that's when birds are most likely to sing. This means he needs to get into position ahead of time, sit perfectly still wearing his false foliage, and wait for the sun to rise or set.

He has to wear his getup so birds won't pay any attention to him, but unfortunately his ambulatory bird blind has the opposite effect on people. When he's in transit to the backcountry to reach his job site, the funny looking suit acts as a visual magnet for tourists.

The same camouflage that makes him invisible to birds renders him terrifying to humans.

Mark's bird-paparazzi work requires stealthy movement (what strangers might interpret as *skulking*), while he's dressed like *Swamp Thing* and carrying a double armload of mysterious-looking electronic equipment.

Let's just say this can cause some confusion.

"Tourists are a real double-edged sword for me," Mark says. "Some of them see my suit and think I'm a poacher, or a terrorist. They call the law on me.

"Other times people are just curious about what I'm doing. But that causes problems, too. A whole family wearing bright orange University of Tennessee t-shirts and ball caps or Hawaiian shirts and board shorts will follow along behind me while I'm trying to sneak up on a bird."

He mimics a crouching tourist high-stepping in a comic book imitation of stealth. "Either way, whether they're afraid of me or just curious, it makes it tough to work.

"Camo is like pepper spray—depending on when and how it's used, it can either repel or attract. "

Mark is a very serious, determined, and focused fellow. He tries not to allow it to be much of an impediment in his life or his work, but he happens to be blind. So he has to have his wife or his brother drive him to the Park and help him get into position.

Once he's there, he likes to be left on his own, but sometimes his intentions for his solo forays don't always work out the way he planned.

"We were in Cades Cove on Hyatt Lane near a field with a Red-shouldered Hawk in it, singing. These hawks will sing for a few seconds, then quit, and then they won't sing again for the whole day.

"They're a really difficult bird, but I wanted to record one of them because the sound is interesting—a Red-shouldered Hawk sounds like a puppy whining.

"I got out of the car and set off with Marci, but she was being cautious walking in the field because the grass was all grown up. My brother Dustin was behind me.

"I got impatient and got ahead of my wife. I was running full bore, holding my microphone out in front of me. I was desperate to get that hawk sound recorded loud and clear, without any ambient noise.

"Marci saw what I needed to do and whispered, 'You're okay, you're not going to hit anything for a hundred feet.' We were out in a huge, flat, open field, so she figured there wasn't much chance for me to get hurt running across it. But she was wrong.

"Later, she told me, 'One second you were there and the next you were gone. You just disappeared! I didn't know what had happened.'

"What happened was I fell into a trench about ten feet wide and six feet deep. It was concealed by the high grass.

"As I fell, I remember thinking, *This is going to be bad. I hope there's no water in whatever it is I'm falling into.* Then I had a brief instant where I felt sorry for myself. I was martyring myself just so other people could get to hear how a Red-shouldered hawk sounded in the wild.

"As I stepped out into mid-air, a voice inside my head said, *One giant leap for mankind.*

"My wife and brother managed to haul me outta the ditch and I wasn't hurt very bad. But in the process, we scared the hawk and it stopped singing, so it was all for nothing."

***

"THE SPOOKIEST PLACE I've ever been in the Park is up Big Creek past Walnut Bottom at Sinking Creek. There's a place there where the creek goes underground. That's why they call is *Sinking Creek.*

"But if you don't know that, as you're walking along, even though you can't see any water, you can still hear it trickling and running. It's creepy even when you do know what's causing the gurgling and gargling sounds."

Joe Kelly

Foreign Bodies

Rick Varner

"I WAS CALLED to deal with a bear on a picnic table. It was the usual—the bear had jumped up to steal a family's meal and chased everyone off.

"Tourists were banging pots and pans, yelling, and banding together to try to run the bear off. The bear wasn't frightened in the least. He'd heard it all before so he went right on eating potato salad.

"Nowadays we have beanbags to shoot the bears with and make them leave without hurting them, but at this time we didn't yet have that option.

"I was trying to figure out what to do when, of a sudden I saw the bear lay its ears back and get a panicked look on its face. I heard a weird sound and the crowd parted.

"A tiny Chinese lady, less than five feet tall, shuffled though the crowd. She was wearing a pointed hat and making a singsong jibber jabber noises. She had four chopsticks in each hand and was clicking them together.

"The bear took a look at her and ran off. He didn't want any of that.

"Bears get used to a certain type of noise and it won't scare them any more, but this was something *very* different.

"To be honest, the sound was so strange, so unexpected, I almost ran away, too."

This Trap's a Snap

Rick Varner

"COUNTING BEARS in the wild isn't easy. It isn't as simple or as relaxing as counting sheep while you lay in bed at night.

"First, you have to find the bears, and that's not easy. One of the techniques used in the counting process relies on humane snares that will capture a bear and hold it temporarily without harming it.

"A student researcher at the University of Tennessee who was using snares to compile bear population estimates was getting extremely frustrated because his traps were being repeatedly robbed of their bait without ever catching a bear.

"This was generating a lot of work for the student, but no useful results for his coursework. He had no choice but to persevere, though, because he needed a good grade, so he hiked out into the backcountry time after time to check and re-bait his empty snares.

"On one of his trips, while he was re-baiting the first of the raided snares on his circuit, a wild black bear came and sat nearby. The bear wasn't acting aggressive. Instead it seemed to be watching him as he worked.

"The college student assumed he was smarter than a bear, so he decided to rig the snare a little differently than he ever had before. When he finished, he backed up out of the way but stayed close enough to see what the bear would do.

"The bear immediately came down the hill to the trap and was able to retrieve the bait, a can of sardines, and eat it without getting caught. Then the bear backed up and waited to see what the college boy would do.

"The student reconfigured the snare and re-baited the trap two more times, and each time the bear stole the bait and ate it while the young man stood nearby and watched in amazement.

"After being humiliated three times in a row, and also realizing he was running low on sardines, the student decided to forget about trying to fool that particular bear. So, he soldiered on through the woods to the location of his next snare to check on it.

"When he arrived at the second trap, the same bear who'd just cleaned him out of three cans of sardines was already there, lying next to the empty snare, waiting for the student to re-bait it so he could have another snack.

"At this point the young man gave up and came to the Wildlife Building to ask for advice.

"I commiserated with him. 'Bears are smart,' I said. 'I've seen them do things I wouldn't have believed were possible if I hadn't been standing there watching them myself.'

"'Once I saw a bear take a rock the size of a bowling ball and roll it down a slope into a trap,' I said. 'The rock hit the snare and set it off. Then the bear went down and stole the sardines.'

"Maybe it was just an accident, but I don't think so. It looked like the bear knew what it was doing. After discussing the options, we were forced to admit defeat. The college boy and the professional wildlife expert were totally outfoxed by that bear."

***

Tourist: "What time do they let the bears out?"

Ranger: "They're out all the time."

Tourist: "What do you mean?"

High-Mileage Hiker

Tom Harrington

"I HIKE A LOT. I used to hike a thousand miles a year. When I stopped keeping track of my mileage it was over 25,000 miles.

"So far I've been charged by bears five times. The first time was scary, but the second time was worse. I was on a long hike after I'd passed three separate signs warning of increased bear activity in the area: one at the beginning of the Anthony Creek Trail, one at the Russell Field Trail junction, and another one at the Bote Mountain Trail junction.

"I picked up a big stick on the Bote Mountain Trail, but kept going. As I came around the last curve where you can see the Appalachian Trail junction, there stood a large bear.

"At the same moment I saw him, he started running toward me. I yelled at him, shook my stick, clapped my hands, and finally started throwing rocks. When I threw the rocks, the bear turned and went into the woods.

"I continued my hike and a few minutes later when I got to Spence Field I saw four men sitting on the ground eating lunch. I called out to tell them about a bear in the area. They turned toward me, looked extremely shocked, and then they all jumped up at the same time and started running.

"One man had taken his boots off while he was resting and he left them behind when he ran away. I thought they were being silly. They didn't need to be *that* scared.

"But then it dawned on me that they might've been reacting to something they were seeing *behind* me. I looked over my shoulder and, sure enough, the bear I thought I'd scared off was racing toward us at full speed.

"The bear ran right past me and went straight for the men's packs where they'd left them on the ground. He tore the packs to shreds, searching for food.

"I looked around, wondering where the men had gone, and saw that all four of them had climbed trees! '*That's* not going to help!' I hollered. 'Bears can climb trees!'

"I decided to leave and ran right on past the trees the men were trying to hide in and made a wide circle back to the trail. Then I resumed my hike, and didn't have any further problems that day.

"I don't know what happened to those men, but I assume they made it out okay because I didn't hear anything about an incident.

"All this trouble happened because hikers had been feeding that bear around the Spence Field Shelter, or leaving scraps in the area, and he'd lost his fear of humans. He'd learned that people had food. Then he discovered they'd throw their packs down and run away if he charged them.

"Learning that was just about the worst thing that could ever have happened to that bear. He'd be nothing but trouble from then on, and, if the rangers couldn't move him away from people, he'll have to be euthanized before he hurt someone.

"I respect bears, but I'm not really afraid of them. The very last thing I'd try in an encounter is giving a bear my pack. I'd only do it when I was absolutely certain that physical contact was imminent."

"I only do day hikes. Uncle Sam broke me from staying out overnight."

"I got a letter from John Fitzgerald Kennedy saying 'You will report to the Armed Forces Induction Station in Knoxville on the first day of May 1963.'

"In boot camp we had to stay out for a week at a time with no baths. They had us put up our tents in the dark and then take them down. Then they made us move down the road half a mile and put them back up again. They were trying to get us ready for Vietnam.

"I didn't have to go, though. They found out I could type and had a college degree, so I ended up spending two years behind a typewriter from 8 a.m. to 5 p.m. about five miles from Camp David.

"Before they'd let anyone go to work there, you had to take a lie detector test, to make sure you wouldn't be vulnerable to blackmail.

"I failed it on the first question—my name. I couldn't understand how that was possible, but they said I'd failed. I told them, 'If that's not my name, I'd like to know what it is!'

"But they stopped the regular test and gave me a whole separate lie detector test with twenty-eight questions just about my *name*. I was able to pass that one.

"Ever since boot camp, I think the best way to hike is to come home at the end of every day to a hot bath and your own bed."

"I was supposed to go hiking on March 13, 1993. It was a friend's birthday and we were supposed to go hiking together. But it turned out to be the day of one of the biggest blizzards ever recorded in the Smokies.

"He called at 6:30 in the morning and said, 'Are you ready to go?'

"I said, 'Have you looked outside?'

"He said, 'I think we can make it.'

"I said, 'You used the wrong pronoun. *You* can make it, not *me*.' I wouldn't go.

"It was so bad, even two weeks later when I tried, I went half a mile through waist high drifts before I'd had enough. My friend didn't want to turn around because he was embarrassed about what the people behind us would think.

"I said, 'I don't care what the people behind us think, I'm going back down.'

"The people behind us had snowshoes on! We didn't. I went back down to a lower elevation and ended up hiking further than my friend did, but not in deep snow.

"Hiking through deep snowdrifts is very, very difficult. It's so strenuous it's like a extremely intensive labor. It takes every ounce of your strength to do *one step*.

"I always keep in mind that when I get to wherever I'm going, I've gotta hike the same distance to get outta there.

"I've climbed Mt. LeConte in the snow when it was so slick I had to crawl. I don't crawl on the ice anymore. I don't go up icy trails anymore. I don't trust clamp-ons. Any of the steep trails will get slick after it snows. The sun will shine on them and melt the snow from underneath and they'll refreeze."

"On the Little Bottoms Trail one Sunday afternoon I refused to go on a hike because the creeks would be up and dangerous. It was a good decision. The washouts were still visible a couple of weeks later. In places like that, you can drown trying to cross, or get trapped on the wrong side of a creek and not be able to get back."

"Once I was hiking on Cooper Road Trail in February. It was fourteen degrees. We came to a big stream crossing with no bridge, but the creek was frozen. The friend I was hiking with is 6'2" and weighs about 230 pounds. He went first and walked across the ice with no problem. Then I followed him and the ice broke under me.

"I went into the creek half way to my knees, both boots were totally underwater. I couldn't understand it. I weighed fifty or sixty pounds less than him! What had happened?

"That's not a hard trail. It's not steep. So I just continued, moving as fast as I could go. After a few minutes the water warmed up inside my boots."

"I went hiking on the Jakes Creek Trail in March with a young teenager and a friend from bible study group. There was snow on ground and no bridge over the creek. 'Give me your car keys,' I said, 'I'm going back to Gatlinburg!'

"But the teenager hopped across that creek on icy rocks. It's a wide creek too. He made it the whole way without falling. So I changed my mind and I took off my boots and waded across. That's probably the stupidest thing I've ever done.

"I was surprised, but after something like that it doesn't take long for your feet to get warm again. In fact, after you dry them and get them back into your boots, they feel like they're on fire. It's the most toasty-warm feeling you can imagine. But then it's painful later.

"That was a bad crossing. A college student drowned there. He had a backpack on and it had rained real hard …."

Tom looked into the distance and stopped speaking. After a moment he added, "Now there's a bridge."

"If you hike in the Smokies you have moss growing between your toes. The high elevations of the Smokies are a temperate rainforest. One year, on the first sixteen Saturdays of the year, I hiked in the rain fourteen times. I don't mind the rain if it's warm, but I don't enjoy it if it's cold.

"I have friends who live in Switzerland who like to hike. I took them to Ramsey Cascade when they came for a visit. It rained on the way back and their whole demeanor changed when they got wet. They had no rain gear. They got real solemn and quiet. I don't think they'd ever gotten that wet during a hike before. I told them they'd had a *Smoky Mountain Baptism*.

"After that they started complaining. They said, 'You speak to everyone on the trail. We don't do that in our country.'

"I said, 'Well we *do* speak to everybody in *our* country, especially this part of it!'"

Where's the Bear?

Rick Varner

"I GOT A CALL saying a bear was in a barn trying to kill someone's calves. It was a nice fall day and I left immediately to see if I could help.

"I got to the farm quick, but didn't see anything going on around the barn. I knocked on the door of the house, and a lady answered it and told me, 'Yeah, the neighbors got together and ran it off. They have it treed in the pasture.'

"I looked where she was pointing and saw a lone tree out in the middle of a field surrounded by men. I still didn't see a bear.

"I walked out into the field and asked one of the men, all of whom were standing there holding rifles or shotguns, 'What've you got in this tree?'

"'He's on the other side,' the fellow said.

"This tree was about eight inches in diameter. I was thinking, *On the other side of what?*

"I walked around the tree and saw a cub that would've weighed maybe twelve pounds.

"The little cub was clinging to the tree less than ten feet off the ground, terrified, trying to stay on the opposite side from the men.

"I climbed up into the tree and stood on a limb and grabbed the little bear. I got him by the scruff of the neck and pulled him off the trunk.

"He bellowed and squalled, but the little thing was an emaciated orphan the size of a beagle.

"A twelve-pound cub will claw your shirt up, or scratch you if you don't keep control of it, but if its mother isn't nearby, it's not a major threat."

"Nevertheless, it was obvious the men thought I was *very* brave. I didn't say anything. I didn't want to hurt their feelings."

Grizzly Bait

Liz Domingue

"I WAS IN YELLOWSTONE National Park and one morning I went to Antelope Creek Valley before dawn to look for bears—grizzlies and black. I knew the bears liked to forage in open meadows, so I went up there with a friend and waited for sunrise.

"A couple drove up and indicated they'd seen a bear so we followed them. Sure enough, there was a grizzly up on the hill out in the open. The bear was about a hundred feet away. All four of us got out to take pictures, but we stayed near our vehicles.

"The forest was behind us. An important rule to remember in dealing with wildlife is—*never* cut off an animal's escape route. And the animal's preferred escape route is not necessarily what most people might expect. It won't simply run away from people. It will seek protection, so it's likely to run toward the woods instead of across an open field.

"When it began to get light, other people could see us, so they pulled over and parked and got out of their cars. Soon there was a long line of cars and a lot of people walking up and down. This was blocking the bear's access to the woods.

"Being out in an exposed field, cut off from a hiding place was making the bear nervous. Unlike with black bears, a grizzly bear encounter has a higher potential to become a dangerous situation.

"The couple we'd followed decided to leave. The man got in their car and was turning it around. I was standing near the back of my Ford Ranger pickup truck, behind a camera mounted on a tripod, watching the bear through my viewfinder.

"Suddenly the bear came loping down the hill. Within the next two or three seconds, my friend and the lady from the couple we'd been talking to hopped into my truck, then some guy I'd never met ran over from the crowd and shoved me out of the way and jumped into the passenger side! I was so shocked I was speechless.

"My truck would only hold three people.

"There I was, holding my camera and tripod, my mouth wide open, and a strange man was sitting inside my truck, leaving me outside with a grizzly bear. At first I couldn't believe it. All I could manage to say was, '*Excuse me!*'

"The guy grabbed my arm and said, 'You can get in, too!'

"I guess I could've if I'd wanted to crowd surf across his lap, but why should I have to leap sideways onto a strangers' lap to get inside my own truck? And there was no way I could do it with a camera and tripod.

"Why wasn't this guy inside his own vehicle?

"Thank goodness I got lucky and the crowd parted and allowed the bear to run into the woods.

"Then, when the bear was out of sight, the man got out of my truck and walked away. As I watched him saunter down the road, all sorts of things began to occur to me, things I wish I'd said, including a lot of foul language, but I didn't say any of it.

"What I learned from that situation was:

1. No matter how good an observer of nature you are, things can change in an instant, and you may not see that change coming.
2. Pay attention to the people around you. Humans are *far* more dangerous and cause *way* more problems than the animals."

Professional Stuffed Animals

WESTY FLETCHER can take the heat. He used to be the manager of the Park store inside the Sugarlands Visitor Center where he handled 825,000 shoppers a year in a space that can comfortably hold a maximum of twenty-four people at a time.

But even Westy has his limits. He reached them during a Fourth of July parade in Gatlinburg. He'd volunteered to ride on a float dressed in a bear costume.

Westy Fletcher

"It was a hot day and I was sweating before the parade even started," he said. "After just a few minutes inside that furry bear suit, I was drenched.

"I'd never sweated so much in my life! Sweat was running in my eyes. I couldn't see *anything*.

"I finally got so overheated I had to take the head off the bear costume for just a second to wipe my eyes. I had to remove the head a couple more times during the parade. It was my bad luck to get on television during one of those brief interludes.

"This made the guy who owned the costume pretty mad. He'd made the loan of the suit subject to only one condition—that I keep the head on at all times.

"I tried my best to stick to our deal, but I just couldn't do it.

"When the parade was over I took the bear costume back. He really read me the riot act. I told him it would've been worse if I'd kept the head on, because then I would've fainted and fallen off the float.

"The sight of a bear, even a fake one, laying in the road during the parade would've been *way* more upsetting to spectators than seeing me wipe my eyes a couple of times! Nobody wants to see a road-kill bear.

"Those bear costumes reek, too," he said, lost in the memory of the parade. "All that sweating …."

"I shoulda known," Westy added, shaking his head. "When the guy gave me the costume, he handed me this spray bottle, and said, 'You have to do something to sanitize the suit.'

"It was a spray bottle of *vodka*. The guy had squirted vodka all over the inside of the suit. He said it was to kill the bacteria.

"Lemme tell ya, when you put that bear head on for the first time, the smell of vodka is overwhelming."

I didn't say anything, but I wondered if maybe sniffing vodka fumes in a confined space helped tranquilize the wearer. Or maybe the whole vodka business was just a cover story concocted by men who had to fortify themselves internally with alcohol before they had the courage to dress up like a bear and cavort in public.

But some good came from the headless bear scandal after all—the Department of Tourism for the City of Gatlinburg decided to spring for an air-conditioned bear costume for the next year's parade.

I suspected Westy was angry about the next guy getting a much nicer suit and I was right. He told me with a bitter edge to his voice that the new bear costume was "a $10,000 model that comes with an internal fan!"

I was stunned. I had no concept for a $10,000 air-conditioned animal costume. My amazement prompted one of my co-workers, Annie, to share some inside information about people who wore fuzzy animal costumes at major sporting events.

"Head mascots get full ride scholarships to college," she said. "That's why students compete for the job."

She made it clear that being a college mascot was no walk in the Park. "It's not as easy as pretending to be a bear while riding a float," she said. "College mascots are really athletic. They have to be in character two hours before a game, all during the event, and for an hour afterwards, constantly moving and engaging the crowd."

"They have to go through all sorts of costume changes, too."

During the recent Homecoming game a friend of hers who was a mascot at a local university wore: (1) a hillbilly costume with overalls and a hat, (2) an Elvis costume with sequined jacket and sequined pants, (3) a mock cheerleader outfit, and (4) a tuxedo with top hat and cane.

And each of these outfits was worn over the top of the animal suit.

Annie's friend, who was near the end of his four years as a college mascot, was hoping to be a mascot for a professional sports team. She said that to make the transition from amateur to pro he'd have to be flexible about the costume.

I wondered if there was a significant difference in pretending to be a Bronco, Buffalo, Oriole, Ram, Native American, or Viking. Were some of the mascots considered more chic than others?

"Why would anyone want to make a *career* out of being a stuffed animal?" I asked, still not getting it. I'd never even imagined the possibility of being a *professional* stuffed animal.

"Because if they're good enough to go pro," Annie said, "they make $150,000 a year and only have to work for six months to get it!"

Ahhh. Now I got it.

The realization that there was huge money to be made in pretending to be a stuffed animal caused me to wonder how much the Gatlinburg bear made.

I called Westy to find out.

Zero, zip, nada…is what Westy got…that and a furious lecture from the guy who loaned him the stinking, vodka-soaked suit.

I told him what pro mascots got paid. He was as shocked as I'd been.

"Would you ever put on a bear suit again?" I asked.

"Sure," he said, "for $150,000. But it would have to be air-conditioned!"

Big Black Hairy Legs

Rick Varner

"I WAS SENT to Balsam Mountain campground to follow up on a report of a large bear approaching folks. The plan was that if I encountered the bear, I should attempt to capture it and, if successful, do a release onsite as a form of aversive conditioning.

"This meant to give the bear a negative experience of being around people—scare it.

"A Student Conservation Association intern was asked to help out and he met me at the campground. We were told the problem bear had been there just minutes before, and were shown where it was last seen.

"We prepared to set the trap I'd brought with me. We pulled it off the trailer and propped the door open, then went about preparing the bait bag—a cotton sack we'd fill with bear goodies. Putting the bait inside a cloth bag gave the bear something to hook his teeth into, and that made it more likely that when he pulled on it, it would trip the trap door and lock him inside.

"I'd brought the traditional bear bait—sardines, along with some bacon, which we've found works great if you have the time to actually fry it onsite. The smell of bacon is one of those universally attractive smells, rivaled only by hot cinnamon rolls!

"I set a small stove on the tailgate of my Park Service truck and was just about to light it, when my helper said he saw the bear coming uphill through the brush—right towards us.

"Since the bear was already on his way, I didn't have time to prepare the bacon, nor did it appear that I'd need it. The animal was only about 100 feet from the trap.

"I grabbed a can of sardines and popped the lid, dumped the contents down into the bait bag, and tied it off. I pushed everything I'd laid out on the tailgate back into the truck bed and closed it.

"The bear had worked his way pretty close to the trap by now, so I shuffled my feet in the gravel to chase him back, to give me the time and room to bait the trap. The bear ran a few yards then stopped to watch what I was doing.

"As I moved closer to the trap, so did he. I yelled, kicked gravel, and charged toward him to get him to back off. He turned and fled, but only about five yards. Then he stopped and watched me go towards the trap—and back he came.

"The idea of crawling into a trap on my hands and knees, while carrying a bag of mushed up sardines, with a very large bear on my heels—especially a bear that was showing a distinct inclination for said sardines, made me pause to rethink my strategies and tactics.

"*Hmmmm.* It looked like this was a situation where a dart gun would be a more effective and safer way to deal with this bear. I returned to the truck, threw the bait bag into the bed, and retrieved my dart gun and drug kit from the cab.

"At the same time, I was doing the math to calculate the correct drug dosage. I estimated the bear's weight at over 200 pounds, so I'd need 4cc, 4ml, of drugs. I started to draw up the dose and I asked my helper to keep an eye on the bear.

"I don't see it anymore," he said. "I think it went back down the hill.

"I thought to myself, *Maybe we'll have to fry some bacon after all.* I had my drug kit laid out on the driver's seat and was standing next to it with the truck door open, mixing the two component drugs that we use for bears.

"I'd just finished the mix, when a movement near my feet caught my attention in my peripheral vision. I looked down and saw two big black hairy legs just on the other side of the truck door, inches from where I stood!

"I'd rather not repeat here what I said when I saw those furry feet right next to mine.

"I jumped up into the truck and slammed the door, then blew the horn. I rolled the window down carefully and peeked out, but I couldn't see the bear. My helper had gone off toward the campground. When he heard the horn toot he realized I must be calling him to come back.

"Do you see the bear anywhere?" I shouted.

"No," the intern said.

"I climbed down out of the truck, picked up a 4 cc dart and the syringe I'd just loaded with the mixed drugs in it. This was not an ideal situation. Transferring the mixed drugs from a syringe into a dart requires good eyesight and, most importantly, steady hands.

"You need to insert the needle on the end of the syringe down inside the needle on the dart and inject the drug into the dart. It's like refueling a jet in mid-air, except with two tiny needles.

"Trying to mate two very small, very sharp objects, one filled with a dose of drugs that would be deadly to a human, is quite stressful even under ideal conditions. Attempting to do it two minutes after discovering a bear almost standing on your toes introduces a whole new level of difficulty.

"After several moments of struggling to *thread the needle* I finally almost had it. And suddenly there the bear was again, at the corner of the truck, coming towards me!

"I shut the truck door and backed around the front corner of the truck, still trying to load my dart, while keeping one eye on the bear. The next time I glanced up I couldn't see the bear. I yelled out to my helper, 'Where you at?'

"'I'm down here," he shouted, "below the bank. I can't find him down here.'

"*No kidding*, I thought. The intern was pretty far away.

"I was standing by the front grill of the truck looking down along the driver's side where I'd last seen the bear, when suddenly I heard a noise behind me. I whirled around and there he was – four feet away!

"I instantly bolted and raced around to the passenger side of the truck, shouting for my helper to get himself back up there and help me. I still had the syringe in one hand and the dart in the other, and I needed to finish loading the dart.

"I finally got it done, but by this time the bear was coming toward me down the driver's side of the truck. My dart gun was still on the driver's seat. A loaded dart wasn't much good without it. I couldn't just throw it at the bear like a game of darts.

"I slowly backed up around the truck and the bear continued to follow me. I kept moving around the vehicle until I got to the driver's side. Then I then raced to the driver's door, jerked it open, grabbed my dart gun, slammed the door, and vaulted up into the bed of the truck.

"My helper came panting up the bank and, at the top, ended up almost face-to-face with the bear. What he said when he realized what he'd done can't be repeated here.

"I suggested he back off, while I figured out what to do.

"The dart guns we used at the time had no way to adjust the power setting to propel the dart. This meant that in order to make a shot without the risk of injuring the animal, the animal needed to be at least thirty feet away.

"I had a real problem. This bear was only *three* feet away, standing on his hind legs, leaning against the bed of the truck, looking like he was gonna join me at any moment.

Think fast Rick! I said to myself.

"I knew that what I wanted to do was going to be counter productive to the plan to aversively condition this bear, but I had to do *something*, so I snatched up the bait bag I'd previously filled with sardines and dangled it over the bear, like a guy at Sea World offering a herring to a seal.

"This got the bear's attention. Then I then threw the bag out into the grass as far away as I could. When the bear went over toward the bait bag, I loaded the dart into the gun and leaned across the cab to get a solid place to rest my hand to steady my aim.

"When the bear stooped down to pick up the bag, I took the shot. The dart hit in a good location and injected the bear with the drugs. The bear bolted a few yards, but then stopped. Then he turned and came back to get his bag of sardines. He laid down and went to sleep with it in his mouth.

"I hoped this would be the end of the problems with this bear, but we had to deal with him again the next year. The second time he wasn't nearly as persistent or scary, just real determined. After the second interaction with us, he decided to stop going near people."

Footloose

Rick Varner

"I WAS GONNA build a bear-proof food storage cable system at a remote campsite. I was ascending a tall tree that had no limbs close to the ground so I was using climbing spikes on my boots. Near the top of the tree, I accidentally kicked too hard and drove one of my spikes in too far.

"I got stuck.

"I couldn't get my foot loose, which meant I couldn't move either up or down. I wasn't wearing a safety harness either, so I had to be careful. It was an embarrassing situation, and also dangerous.

"I couldn't untie my boot and step out of it because I needed both boots and both spikes to climb back down to safety. And I couldn't use my hands to try to pull myself loose because I couldn't let go of the tree.

"It was incredibly awkward. If I could manage to get my boot off I'd still have to reach a branch sturdy enough to sit on and wait up in the tree until someone came by. That would be a *really* long and miserable wait.

"But even if someone wandered by, what could they do? They'd have to go get someone to come up there with rope and tools to help me down. Clearly, I needed to get myself loose while I still had the strength to do it.

"To get enough leverage to pull the jammed spike loose, I was gonna have to kick my other foot in real tight, too.

"There's a risk in doing that. You hope you don't end up with both feet stuck at the same time.

"I was lucky and eventually I managed to tear myself free, but it was pretty awkward hugging that tree way up in the air, wondering what I was gonna do if I couldn't get *either* foot loose."

Bear in the Air

Rick Varner

"ONE SATURDAY I came to work and noticed a co-worker's personal truck was parked down at the Wildlife Building. That was a little unusual, so I decided to see what was going on.

"As soon as I turned the knob on the front door, it came flying open, and one of the wildlife rangers, Kim DeLozier, staggered back a half step onto the stoop. Obviously he'd been leaning hard against the door when I opened it.

"I looked into the room and saw why.

"He was holding a bear by the ears and was struggling to keep its face pinned down against the gurney where we lay bears while we work on them. Apparently the bear had woken up unexpectedly and wanted to get out of there.

"Kim was repeating over and over in a calm voice, 'Jennifer get some drugs … Jennifer get some drugs.'

"But his assistant, Jennifer, was standing in the corner of the room, paralyzed with shock.

"The bear was coming wider awake and getting more vigorous in its efforts to get loose. Its rear end was sticking way up in the air and it was using its hind feet to push against the table and head-butt Kim.

"There was no room to squeeze past Kim and the bear in the doorway, so I ran around the building to the back door and came up behind the bear and grabbed its back feet.

"That helped, but then Kim and I were stuck holding a squirming eighty-pound bear up in the air between us!

"We weren't going to be able to control the situation for long.

"I hollered, 'Jennifer, *please* load up a syringe and shoot this bear!'

"Thank goodness she was able to recover her wits then and she prepared a syringe and got the bear sedated again.

"It's funny now, but I tell ya, it was a fairly intense few minutes while Kim and I had to hold an unhappy bear in the air between us."

The Pear-Shaped Bear

Rick Varner

"EXPERTS SAY if a bear can manage to get its head through a hole, it'll be able to get its whole body out through it.

"All of our hog traps have a ten-by-ten-inch escape hole built into them so small animals like raccoons or bobcats can get out if they get locked inside. A bear can't normally get through a ten-inch hole. But bears are sometimes strong enough to tear their way out of a chain link cage if they have enough time.

"I checked a hog trap one day and found a large bear trying to escape. This bear was particularly heavy in the hindquarters. His head and one arm were sticking out of the little escape hole, but it was obvious, at least to me, that there was no way he was gonna be able to get his 300-pound rear end through that little hole.

"He was stuck tight and was using his free arm to rip at the chain link.

"I needed to help the bear out of his predicament, but I wasn't really sure how to do it without coming into contact with his claws. My first idea was to get a stick and pop him on the nose to try to get him to pull his head back out of the hole.

"I tried it, but that didn't help. He didn't move backwards. Instead he wanted to fight with the stick. Next I moved around behind him and poked him in the butt.

"When I did that he arched his body and jammed himself further into the small hole. I tried it again anyway, thinking he'd back up out of the escape hole so he could turn around and face me, but it just made the situation worse.

"What the bear really needed to do was to scrunch down into a position like an abdominal crunch. I pondered how to get him to do this.

"I decided the best way to get him to contract his abs would be to pull on the fur on his stomach.

"I reached into the trap and tugged at the fur on his belly. This worked. The bear scrunched down and got about half way back out of the hole. His head was out now to the ears. He almost got me with his free paw, too.

"I needed to do it again, but I didn't dare use my hand this time, so I broke off a sapling tree and frayed it into a star on one end. I stuck it through the chain link and twisted it against the bear's stomach.

"It worked again. I used the stomach stick three times in all and the bear got himself completely unstuck and back down into the main part of the cage. As soon as he was all inside, I lifted the door and he ran off.

"The last part of him that disappeared into the woods was his big rear end."

Bear Beware

Rick Varner

"WE USED TO HAVE a lot of bear problems at popular picnic areas. The situation is much better nowadays, but it used to be common for bears to interfere with family meals. At lunchtime there might be half a dozen bears hanging around a picnic area at the same time.

"The way things used to be, before we starting paying attention to garbage and educating people to not leave *anything* where bears could get to it, a bear would see a family having a picnic and he'd leap right up onto the middle of the table and start eating anything and everything.

"One year a Student Conservation Association intern was working near one of the picnic areas when he heard a big racket and glanced up just in time to see a mother and her two daughters run past, screaming hysterically.

"He took off running in the opposite direction, toward where the women had come from, to see what the problem was. A bear was on a picnic table gobbling a family's lunch.

"Everybody had bolted from table except for a very elderly man whose walker had been set off to one side—out of his reach.

"Because the 90 year old fellow couldn't get to his walker and was too frail to stand up without it, he was trapped alone at the table with the bear.

"The gentleman wasn't doing anything threatening, but he was close enough to the food to annoy the bear. The bear didn't want to share, so he leaned right into the old man's face and growled and snapped his jaws to scare him away.

"The bear's tactic was very effective. Great grandpa was certainly afraid. He fell backwards and would've fallen off the bench and out of the way, but his feet got tangled up underneath the picnic table.

"He was trapped with his rear end still on the picnic bench, but with his torso stretched out away from the table.

"Unfortunately, he still wasn't far enough away to satisfy the bear.

"Lucky for the old man, the SCA intern was a brave fellow.

"The intern saw that the spectators, a big crowd which included the elderly gentleman's entire family, were all too frightened to do anything to help the old man, so the intern ran up to the table and did the only thing he could think of.

"He punched the bear right in the nose.

"And it worked! The bear ran off.

"The young man helped the old fellow get his legs sorted out and sit up. He was shaken, but not hurt. The boy brought the walker close to the bench and helped the man get up. At this point the family took over and helped great grandpa begin to make his way back to the car.

"I've always thought that must've been a real awkward ride back home inside that family's car after every last one of them had abandoned one of their own to the mercy of a wild animal.

"The intern thought this was a happy ending for everyone, but some of the people who'd been watching the show took offense at his behavior.

"The Park got four reports of a man assaulting a bear before the intern could reach his boss to explain what had happened."

Sleeping With Bears

Rick Varner

"I'D BEEN WORKING all night and went into one of the cabins at Le Conte Lodge to take a nap before hiking back down the mountain.

"Something woke me up and I rolled over to discovered a bear right next to me. I immediately rolled back away from the bear and, at the same time, it took off out the door.

"I scrambled up and went to the door of the cabin to see where the bear had gone. He hadn't gone far. He was right there at the door.

"Before I could understand what was happening, the bear shoved me back inside. He put one paw on my chest and one on my groin, and shoved me down, then came right over the top of me headed for the trashcan inside the cabin.

"I kicked him and the bear ran away again, but he only went about ten feet. Then he came back to the stoop of the cabin and sat down and looked right at me, like a dog.

"I looked back at the bear and we both tried to stare each other down.

"When I stared hard, the bear would look away. But then the bear tried to squeeze past me in the doorway, real gently, without making eye contact. He tried a couple of times to ease around me, but I kept thwarting him gently.

"Then something about the bear's eyes changed and he suddenly went for me and knocked me backwards again. I kicked him again and he ran off.

"I stayed at the cabin to see if he came back. Sure enough, he didn't leave the area. An hour later he bluff charged a bunch of people who'd gathered around him in a circle to take pictures. He backed off when he saw me coming.

"Two hours later the bear went inside another one of the cabins. This one had three little girls inside about eight or ten years old. They were crying, all of them bunched up together in the top bunk while the bear ate their trail mix on the lower bunk.

"I kicked the bear off the bed, and kicked him on out the door. He rolled down the steps and disappeared into the briars. But he didn't stop. Instead he went to the shelter that's an eighth of a mile above the Lodge.

"He approached people repeatedly. He'd sweep the crowd to see if he could get any food, then he'd fade back into the brush.

"I wanted to gauge his aggressiveness, so the next time he came toward the crowd, I acted like I was scared, on purpose, to see what he'd do. The bear came for me instantly. This time I had to hurt him to get him to back off.

"The next day Kim DeLozier hiked up to the top of the mountain and euthanized him. We didn't like to have to do this, but the bear had gotten too dangerous, even at his small size. When he got bigger he would be fearsome.

"This bear struck a girl with his paw, so he couldn't ever be allowed to continue this behavior."

"Early notification is the essential to save a bear like this. You can't let things progress too far or there's no recourse but putting the bear down.

"We had to euthanize a bear this year that had been visiting an area for weeks before it eventually broke into a building. The people could've nipped it in the bud, but their customers like to see bears, so they didn't discourage it until things got very dangerous.

"I try to look for some good to come out of things like this. I think the people who were involved learned to not allow things to escalate. If it happens again, they'll call us early.

"Unfortunately, the bears had to pay the ultimate price for their lesson."

"Cabin rental people will sometimes put trash out on a porch either in ignorance or because they hope a bear will come investigate so they can see it up close. They don't think about the future of the bear or of other guests at that cabin. And they don't realize, if they've left a window open, the bear might just come on inside because he smells more food in there."

Hudgens Hell

Joe Kelly

"MOST OF THE PARK is a very formidable wilderness.

"You learn how rough it is when you're out searching for people who've gotten lost. Even as a professional, you can start out *searching* but then find your self in a situation where you forget everything but *surviving*!

"I participated in several rescues that got tough. One was in a place called Hudgen's Hell—the name says it all.

"It's on the backside of Mt. LeConte off Alum Cave Trail near Styx Branch—and again, the name Styx says loads. The whole area is a rough terrain with a terrible tangle of rhododendron and mountain laurel shrubs that are nearly impenetrable.

"When we set out, it was extremely cold, but it was dry. But as we hiked higher it began to rain. We gained some more altitude and the rain turned to sleet, and then to snow. And then the snow got *deep*.

"At one point all I could think was, 'Lord, take me home!'

"It's so steep and dense with shrubbery you can't really *fall down* but you can never really *get up* either. You just scrabble and scramble the whole time.

"Inside the hell itself, it would've been easier if I could've gotten down on my hands and knees and crawled out underneath the bushes using the tunnels the bears had made, but on that day they were filled with snow!

"The only way you can progress through these places is to fling yourself forward, or try to climb up onto the top of the rhododendron bushes and lay sideways and roll across the top of them as far as you can, until you reach a gap in the vegetation.

"Then you go crashing down through the branches and have to climb back up through the tangle of roots and branches again to get on top of it and keep hurling your self forward somehow.

"Coming down out of a place like that you need hobnails in the seat of your pants.

"The only reason you go in there is because you know a hiker is gonna die if you don't get to them as soon as possible. But by the end of a trip like this you're wondering if any of you are gonna make it out alive."

The EmBEARrassed Bear

Rick Varner

"WE WERE HAVING bear problems in Cades Cove in a grove of white oak trees. The grove was a bear magnet because of the acorns. I once saw thirteen bears there in a single afternoon.

"We were gonna have to catch and move a mother bear with two cubs because she'd been bluff charging people.

"In the early days we tried to catch the momma first, but if we couldn't catch the cubs, we'd have to let her go. Later we learned to get the cubs first because the mother bear will usually stay close by and we can catch the whole family easier that way.

"This time we approached the family and charged at the cubs to try to get them to go up in a tree. If we could keep them there, we could dart them with a pistol and then dart the mother.

"As Kim DeLozier and I were running the cubs up a tree, the momma bear got hot about it and kept bluff charging us.

"'You keep Momma off me,' Kim said, 'and I'll get a jab pole and get these cubs.'

"I had an armload of sticks and was throwing them at the mother bear to try to drive her back, but she kept coming close to us. I'd throw a stick and she'd go up a tree and stop a couple of feet off ground.

"I stood there watching her. After a minute she'd jump back down onto the ground. Then I'd throw a stick to make her jump up onto the side of the tree trunk and she'd hang on there for a minute or two while Kim tried to dart her cubs.

"We repeated this five or six times. I'd chase her up into the tree, but she wouldn't go high up. She kept jumping down, trying

91

to run toward her cubs, and I kept having to throw a stick to get her to go back onto the tree.

"I looked over toward Kim to see what his status was when I had my head turned she got about six feet away from the tree. Kim saw what she was doing and whooped at her real loud.

"That scared her and she whirled around and leaped up, but she'd forgotten that this time she was farther away from the tree than she'd been before, so when she jumped, she missed the tree totally.

"Instead she grabbed a big armful of nothing. Both paws swatted through the air and she ended up grabbing her own shoulders in a bear hug.

"She got this funny look on her face, like she was embarrassed. Then she hopped over to the tree and climbed up a couple of feet like she had before.

"It was so funny—the bear was obviously embarrassed. You wouldn't think animals would get embarrassed, but they do."

Dead Batteries

Dwight McCarter

"THE MATING SEASON for bears is from around the last week of May to the first week of June. During that time, as for any large wild animal during mating season, it's best not to annoy them. Smart people stay far, far away from them.

"Part of the University of Tennessee's long-term research on black bears is to track them with battery-powered radio collars to learn about where the bears forage and hibernate, and all sorts of other interesting things.

"One of the students who was working in the bear project noticed that the batteries were failing in one of the collars. He decided he should go find the bear and exchange the weak batteries for fresh ones.

"Unfortunately this was during the middle of the bears' mating season.

"The student had been told by his professor that it wasn't a good time to attempt to catch a bear, but he knew if he waited until mating season was over, the batteries were likely to be completely dead. If that happened, no one would ever be able to find that bear again.

"So the young man was stuck between the proverbial rock and a hard place.

"He came to me because he'd heard I had some experience with difficult animal encounters and talked me into going with him to the find the bear—to see if together we could figure out a way to replace the batteries.

"I was *very* reluctant to participate in this endeavor, but the student was desperate and begged me, so I loaded up a tranquilizer rifle and we set off hiking together.

"As we got closer to the source of the signal, I realized we were approaching a favorite mating area of the bears—a place nicknamed *The Dance Floor*.

"The Dance Floor is a large flat area atop a ridge in an isolated area of the Park. It was known to be a place where male bears would gather and try to attract the favorable attention of a female bear.

"When we got close enough to lay eyes on the particular bear we were looking for, we discovered he was only one of *eight* male bears showing off in front of a female bear who was apparently pretty hard to impress.

"The bears were putting on a fantastic display to demonstrate their agility and courage, climbing up trees very fast, flipping over and running back down again, and having mock battles. The scene was like a singles bar for bears.

"Only one of the males was wearing a radio collar, so we were certain we'd found the bear we were looking for.

"I was hanging back as far as possible, having absolutely no intention of getting involved in such a volatile situation. The inexperienced student, however, was not deterred. He asked me, 'Are you gonna shoot him?'

"I shook my head.

"'Why not? He's just right over there!'

"'Are you out of your mind?' I said. 'Say I get a good shot and he falls down for a few minutes, how're you gonna get close enough to him to change out the batteries in his collar?'"

"'Can't you go in there and drag him out so I can work on him?' the student asked.

"'Hell no!' I said, 'I'd like to see *you* go in there and try to drag him out of the middle of that bunch!'

"Although we were whispering, our heated discussion began to attract the attention of the bears and the animals didn't welcome the distraction.

"'Here, let me have the rifle,' said the student. 'I'll take the shot. I'll shoot the female and once she's out of commission, the males will disperse and we can load up another dart and shoot the one wearing the collar.'

"'Son,' I said, 'you don't seem to understand. If you dart *her* and she passes out, you've just closed down the most popular floorshow in town. You're gonna make enemies. Then eight really disappointed male bears are gonna come looking for you.'

"The student still wasn't convinced, so I added, 'If you don't make a perfect shot, but just manage make her angry or afraid, and she doesn't go down, *nine* bears will come after us.'

"The student thought about this for a few seconds and then realized I was probably right. We crept away from *The Dance Floor* as quietly as possible."

***

"PARK STATISTICS reveal that ninety percent of Park visitors never get more than fifty feet from their cars. For most people it's a drive-thru wilderness. That's a shame."

Tom Harrington

Bear-Induced Amnesia

Jack Burgin

"MY DAD, my brother, and I were on a three-day hike.

"We'd made it almost to the shelter at Icewater Springs on the Appalachian Trail. Both my brother and I were wearing backpacks with food in them.

"A female bear suddenly appeared between us and the shelter. You could tell she was sizing us up, thinking *Backpack = Food*.

"She seemed to be trying to decide which one of us she should attack to see if she could take our pack, or scare us into giving it to her.

"After several long and terrifying moments, she picked me, and charged. And let me tell you, it was scary.

"Despite everything I knew and everything I'd been told, I did the wrong thing. I ran.

"Then I made another bad decision. I ran to the nearest tree and climbed it.

"The bear walked over to the base of the tree, looked up at me, and then started up after me.

"To this day I still have no memory of what happened next. I was so terrified that I have honestly have amnesia about it.

"I know that somehow I managed to get down out of that tree—and that means I *had* to have passed the bear—but I have no idea how I was able to do it.

"I can remember what happened right *after* I got out of the tree. I remember running into the shelter and slamming the door behind me, but that's all.

"There's a gap in my memory that I've never been able to retrieve.

"When I got inside the shelter I still had my pack on and my dad and my brother were already in there.

"That bear could've *taken* my pack if she wanted to. She could've *torn me up*. A bear's claws are really huge and bears are immensely strong. But she didn't hurt me.

"I don't know why she chased *me* and left my father and brother alone. They, of course, thought the whole thing was hilarious, but the experience wasn't as enjoyable for me.

"I've always been glad I didn't give that bear my pack.

"If I had, she'd have been rewarded for her aggression toward a human. A bear that's gotten that sort of positive reinforcement for aggression is a potential danger to every person she gets near.

"No one should ever give a bear their pack unless there's no alternative."

Changes

Joe Kelly

"THERE'VE BEEN a lot of changes over the years in how we interact with the animals and the natural environment in the Smokies. My favorite observation about the changes came from one of our older rangers.

"This fellow lived at a remote station in Cataloochee where the Park Service decided to add a little public picnic area. I happened to be over there when the maintenance people were installing the picnic tables in his yard.

"He said, 'In my day we ate in the house and went to the restroom in the yard. Nowadays people eat outside and go to the restroom in the house! Don't talk to me about progress!'"

The Story of Mr. Woo

Dwight McCarter

"THE ENTIRE WOO FAMILY, Mr. and Mrs. Woo and their two children, from Osaka, Japan, came to the Smokies and spent a night up in the highest elevations of the Park at the exclusive Le Conte Lodge.

"A mother bear lived within a few miles of the Lodge and was well known to hikers. They'd named her Sheba and they called her cub Timmy. Every day at dawn Sheba liked to browse in the vegetation alongside the trail that led to the Lodge. Momma bear stayed on the ground grazing, while baby bear took a nap safely up in a nearby tree.

"The Woo family decided to leave the Lodge at about the same time Timmy finished his nap and came down from the tree to play. Mr. Woo was an avid photographer. He took lots of snapshots as the family made their way down the mountain.

"After a few miles the Woo family reached the place where Timmy was playing in the trail. They were fascinated to see a real live black bear cub. Mr. Woo approached to within a few feet of Timmy to take some close-ups. This scared Timmy and he bawled for his momma.

"Sheba rushed to her cub's side at her top speed of roughly thirty-three miles an hour. Mr. Woo never saw her coming because he had his back to her, clicking away with his camera.

"Sheba slammed into Mr. Woo hard, intending to knock him away from Timmy. The impact with the angry mother bear sent Mr. Woo airborne off the low side of the trail while his family looked on in horror.

"Mr. Woo took Sheba's warning very seriously and once he hit the ground, he continued to run down the steep hill, off-trail through the woods, as fast as he could go. Unfortunately his running away provoked a chase reflex in Sheba and she took off after him.

"Eventually Mr. Woo ran so far he went beyond the limits of Sheba's territory and, as soon as he did, she stopped chasing him and ran back up the hill to see about her baby.

"Of course, Mr. Woo didn't realize that he'd gotten outside Sheba's territory, or that she'd stopped chasing him, so he kept running. Meanwhile, back up on the trail, Mrs. Woo and the two children were left alone and were even more terrified than Timmy the cub.

"They didn't know what to do. They moved well away from the cub and waited, but Mr. Woo didn't come back. Eventually, the remnants of the Woo family continued down the mountain and made it to the highway off Alum Cave Trail where they found a ranger—me.

"Unfortunately, they couldn't explain what had happened because none of them spoke any English. To communicate, Mrs. Woo drew a set of pictures of the mother bear, the cub, the trail, Mr. Woo, and generally made it clear what had happened by means of a homemade comic strip that looked a lot like *The Far Side*, except it was true.

"At this point the Woo's luck changed for the better. They'd come to the right person. I was one of the Park's best trackers.

"I hot-footed it up Alum Cave Trail and after about three and a half miles I found Timmy up in a tree bawling. I saw Mr. Woo's camera beside the trail and noticed broken vegetation leading downhill into the woods.

"From there I followed skid marks in the dirt and leaves to where the signs indicated Sheba had turned around and gone back to her cub. I continued to track Mr. Woo until finally I spied him sitting several yards away on a rock.

Mr. Woo was still overwrought, so when he heard my approach, despite my assurances, he ran from me, crashing even farther away through the brush. This behavior isn't uncommon in the Park among hysterical lost people, so I wasn't totally surprised.

"I ran after him. By the time I was able to catch up and tackle him, Mr. Woo had a gash over his eye and an impressive assortment of scrapes and bruises.

"I administered first aid, then escorted Mr. Woo down Trout Branch and reunited him with his family. Everyone was mightily relieved—the Woos, Sheba, Timmy, and me.

"The Woo family returned to Osaka and the bear family remained in their home territory near the Lodge.

"I'VE SPENT YEARS hiking in the wilderness and I'm not scared of bears or snakes. I'm scared of people.

"In my experience, animals will run away if they smell you, or hear, or see you, even bears or wild hogs.

"People won't do that. Especially ones who mean you harm."

Liz Domingue

A FREQUENT TOPIC of conversation among the most experienced hikers in the Smokies concerns which things are actually dangerous and which are not.

There is general agreement that two of the most formidable threats are come from unexpected sources.

"Cotton kills!" they say.

Cotton is infamous for contributing to hypothermia because it gets wet from sweat or rain and retains moisture. This can become deadly in higher elevations in the Park or whenever temperatures fall quickly.

"Yellow jackets are the real alpha predators of the Smokies."

There are far more deaths from anaphylactic shock from stings than from bears. And far more trips to the hospital are caused by yellow jackets than bears. When you think about it in terms of sheer numbers, an attack from a nest of bees or other stinging insects can dwarf the number of mammals or reptiles you might encounter.

Bear in the Back Seat 3

Dwight McCarter

IN KEEPING with the tradition started in the *Bear in the Back Seat* books—a multi-volume *Wall Street Journal* best selling series with wildlife ranger Kim DeLozier—here is yet another true story featuring a wild black bear that surprises a driver by unexpectedly appearing in the back seat of his car.

"Because of the rough terrain in the Southern Appalachian Highlands, roads tend to be tortuous. The curving can sometimes get extreme as it does along the southwest border of the Great Smoky Mountains National Park where there's a world famous stretch called *The Dragon* that has 318 turns in an eleven-mile stretch.

"Inside the national park itself there are very few roads. The biggest of these is a two-lane stretch that runs through half a million acres of wilderness for thirty-five-miles—from Gatlinburg, Tennessee to Cherokee, North Carolina. This route, Hwy. 441, crosses the spine of the Smoky Mountains, the Appalachian Trail, and the Tennessee-North Carolina state line at Newfound Gap.

"There are splendid vistas of the Smokies from the gap and at many places along Hwy. 441. These views attract millions of people, so it's impossible for the rangers to keep an eye on everything that happens. But when the situation gets well and truly out of hand, someone will eventually call a ranger to come fix it.

"One of the dumbest things that ever happened on the main road through the Park was when two young fellows decided they'd like to make a pet out of a wild black bear, so they drove into the Park to catch one. They put a modest amount of thought into the endeavor and worked out what they figured was a foolproof plan.

"They drove to a parking lot and opened the trunk of their car. Then they put a bucket of chicken inside and removed the lid from the bucket so the smell of fried chicken could waft on the breeze.

"They moved off to one side and waited for a bear to come looking for the chicken. Before too long an unsuspecting solitary adult male bear smelled the delicious odor of the chicken, wandered over to the car, and obligingly climbed into the trunk to enjoy the lunch that had been set out.

"At first, the men's plan seemed to be working perfectly. They sneaked back to their car, slammed the trunk lid to trap the bear inside, and then drove off, heading for home.

"They congratulated themselves on a job well done. They'd captured *their very own bear*! And it had all been so easy.

"It took about five minutes for a flaw in their plan to become obvious. They'd seriously underestimated the strength and determination of a frightened, angry bear, and the use he could make of his formidable claws and teeth.

"They'd also vastly overestimated the durability of the wall between the trunk and the passenger compartment of their car. Suddenly they found themselves having to deal with one heck of a back seat driver.

"The two fellows weren't prepared to deal with an enraged bear in the back seat, so they decided to abandon their plan—and their car.

"The driver swerved to the side of the road and jammed the gearshift into park. Both boys leaped out and slammed the doors behind them so the bear couldn't give chase. Then they ran away.

"This left an interesting spectacle on Hwy. 441.

"Carload after carload of tourists went motoring past a vehicle that had a bear loose inside the passenger compartment. Nobody knew what to make of it.

"Eventually the bear moved from the back seat to the driver's seat, and this looked even more bizarre. It looked sorta like a bear might be touring the Park in his own car.

"The sight made an extremely strong impression on all the families who passed by. The situation was reported at the Visitors Center *many* times. After the first report a ranger was immediately dispatched to the scene to see what the heck was going on.

"The ranger confirmed that a wild black bear was indeed inside a car sitting alongside the highway. He wasn't exactly sure how the bear got into a closed vehicle, but it was clear that the creature wanted out.

"The ranger stopped the traffic in both directions for the bear's safety and approached the car to free the poor victim of a bear-napping. As soon as he opened a door, the terrified bear bolted for safety—thrilled to be able to get back to the woods after its first and, one hopes its last, ride through the Park.

"Luckily the bear was unharmed.

"The same cannot be said for the interior of the car.

"After the ranger freed the bear, he examined the vehicle where he found the remnants of the bucket of chicken in the area that used to be the trunk, and was able to reconstruct the events.

"He decided to use tactics similar to the bear-nappers and he left the car where it was, but moved out of sight and waited for the owners to return for what was left of their car.

"When they did, he arrested them.

"The bear didn't cause any further trouble.

"Were the two poachers smarter than the average bear? Not even close."

About the Author

4-Time Wall Street Journal best selling author of heartwarming and heartbreaking memoir, biography, and mystery. Carolyn Jourdan chronicles miracles, mayhem, comedy, tragedy, and madcap medical moments in Appalachian medicine, as well as zany and touching interactions with wildlife in the Great Smoky Mountains National Park.

Jourdan's trademark blend of wit and wisdom, humor and humanity have earned her high praise from Dolly Parton and Fanny Flagg, as well as major national newspapers, the New York Public Library, Elle, Family Circle Magazine, and put her work at the top of hundreds of lists of best books of the year and funniest books ever.

Carolyn is a former U.S. Senate Counsel to the Committee on Environment and Public Works and the Committee on Governmental Affairs. She has degrees from the University of Tennessee in Biomedical Engineering and Law. She lives on the family farm in Strawberry Plains, Tennessee, with many stray animals.

Carolyn's first book: "Heart in the Right Place" is a #7 Wall Street Journal best seller and #1 in Biography, Memoir, Science, Medicine, and Doctor-Patient Relations on Amazon.

The follow-up, "Medicine Men: Extreme Appalachian Doctoring," is a #5 and #6 Wall Street Journal best seller and #1 in Biography, Memoir, Science, Medicine, and Doctor-Patient Relations on Amazon, as well as an Amazon All-Star.

"Bear in the Back Seat: Adventures of a Wildlife Ranger in the Great Smoky Mountains National Park" is a #9 Wall Street Journal best seller and #1 in Science, Biology, Animals, Bears, and Travel Biography on Amazon.

"Bear Bloopers: True Stories from the Great Smoky Mountains National Park" is Jourdan's most recent book of true escapades of black bears and rangers in the Great Smoky Mountains National Park.

"Out on a Limb: A Smoky Mountain Mystery," is a #6 in the USA best seller and #1 in Mystery, Cozy Mystery, and Medical Fiction on Amazon.

Visit her at www.CarolynJourdan.com and hear her read stories from her books.

http://facebook.com/CarolynJourdan

http://facebook.com/CarolynJourdanAuthor

http://twitter.com/CarolynJourdan